Contents

Preface

Side by Side Chinese & English Grammar presents the essential elements of Chinese grammar—usually covered in a high school program or in the first year of college Chinese—"side by side" with their English counterparts. This comparative/contrastive approach allows students to build on what they already know, as they see the ways in which English and Chinese are similar and different, and to avoid potential trouble spots.

Side by Side Chinese & English Grammar can be used as

1. a reference book for beginning students, for whom the standard works are too complex to be useful. This allows students a means for independent inquiry.

2. a means of quick review of material forgotten over the summer or material covered in a missed class.

3. a means of helping a student in a new school catch up with the class.

4. a means of organizing or summarizing material presented in the primary text, especially for students whose learning style favors an "organized approach."

5. a means of providing a common background for talking about language with students who have studied English in different ways, so that their study of Chinese will show them something about how language works.

6. an alternative method of explaining grammatical points in both English and Chinese.

Special features of the book that students will find useful include

1. a standard format that introduces each part of speech and answers the most common questions about it.

2. Quick Check charts that allow students to express themselves with more confidence, since they can independently check their sentences against a model.

3. an exercise section (with an answer key) that tests understanding of the main grammatical areas covered in the book.

4. pinyin transliteration, provided for all words presented in the simplified version of Chinese characters.

5. English translations of all Chinese examples.

We hope that this text will provide ways for students to increase their independent work and to adapt material to their own learning styles and situations.

Introduction

The purpose of this book is to help you learn Chinese more easily.

Many students have had trouble with foreign languages because they have not looked carefully enough, or critically enough, at their own. Struggles with your own language took place at such an early age that you may have forgotten the times when it seemed difficult. Now it seems perfectly natural to you, and it is hard to adapt to different ways of expressing ideas.

You may have heard that Chinese is a difficult language to learn. However, this book will show you that, in many ways, Chinese is easier than English. For example, Chinese verbs do not change form in different tenses, and Chinese nouns do not have separate singular and plural forms.

The material in this book has been classified and arranged to show you English and your new language "side by side." Information that is the same for both English and Chinese is usually not repeated on facing pages. If you find that a section is omitted for the Chinese, look to your left and find it on the English page. In many cases, the examples in Chinese match the English examples on the left-hand page.

Why grammar?

People can speak, read, or write their native language, at least to a reasonable degree, without studying formal grammar (the rules governing how we say, change, and arrange words to express our ideas). Just by being around other speakers, we hear millions of examples, and the patterns we hear become a part of us. Even babies start with correct basic patterns (subject-verb-object), even though words may be missing or incorrect: "Me wants cookie!"

Knowledge of grammar helps a great deal, though, in testing new and more complex words or patterns and in analyzing one's writing to discover where a sentence went wrong or how it could be more effective. Sometimes, "It sounds right (or wrong)" won't help.

All of the explanations in this book reflect standard English and Chinese. You may sometimes think, "I don't say that!" The important word here is "say." We often ignore some rules in conversation, or even in informal writing such as friendly letters. When you are writing an important paper or giving a speech, however, you may want to use the standard form in order to make the best possible impression. You will also find that knowing grammar will help you in your study of language.

In learning a foreign language, grammar is necessary because it tells you how to choose the right word—or the right form of a word that you are using for the first time. It is not the way that you acquired your native language as a child, but it is an efficient way for adults who want to express more complex ideas and do not want to make any more mistakes than absolutely necessary.

Grammar saves you time and prevents many mistakes by guiding you in your choices.

Introducing languages

A short history of English

What we now know as England was settled in the fifth and sixth centuries AD by Germanic tribes like the Angles, the Saxons, and the Jutes—all speaking related, but distinct, dialects. Later, in the ninth century, Scandinavian invaders came, bringing their languages, which also contributed to English. Political power determined the centers of learning, which contained the literature of continental Europe, written in Latin, as well as contributions of the inhabitants of Britain. By the ninth century, the primary center was in Wessex, due to the Viking invasions in the north, and so the West Saxon dialect became standard as Old English. It was heavily inflected, with endings on nouns to show many cases and on verbs to show time and person.

This was the language current in 1066, when William the Conqueror, from the province of Normandy in what is now France, won the battle of Hastings and became ruler of England. The natives knew no French; William and his followers did not speak Old English. For a long time, each group continued to speak its own language, but gradually they merged. Since the governing group spoke French, we often find that words for work, home, and ordinary things come from Old English, while words for leisure or artistic goods come from French.

Wamba, the jester in Sir Walter Scott's *Ivanhoe,* made a joke about this, saying that cows and pigs were Anglo-Saxon while the peasants took care of them, but became French (beef and pork) when they were ready to be eaten. In the same way, "house" looks and sounds like the German word *Haus,* but "mansion" looks like the French word for "house," *maison.*

English often uses several words with a similar meaning, with the more elegant word frequently being of French origin. For example, instead of "give," we may say "donate," which is like the French *donner*; instead of "mean," we may say "signify," from French *signifier.*

Latin, the language of the church and therefore of learning in general throughout all Europe, also had an influence on English. Around 1500, English absorbed about 25 percent of known Latin vocabulary. English, therefore, is basically a Germanic language, but one to which large portions of French and Latin were added.

Since the French also borrowed from Latin in the Renaissance, the languages have many words in common, but they are not the everyday words. Compare the following.

GERMANIC ROOT (COMMON)	FRENCH ROOT (ELEGANT)	LATIN ROOT (LEARNED)
ask	*question*	*interrogate*
goodness	*virtue*	*probity*
better	*improve*	*ameliorate*
rider	*cavalier*	*equestrian*

A short history of Chinese

The Chinese language has existed for more than 3,000 years. The earliest records of Chinese date back to the Shang dynasty (1600–1050 BCE). Chinese belongs to the Sino-Tibetan language family, together with Burmese, Tibetan, and many languages spoken in Southeast Asia and parts of South Asia.

Unlike Latin, which absorbed features of other languages as it spread across Europe and evolved into French, Italian, and the other Romance languages, there has only been one written form of Chinese throughout its history; this form is used for literary texts, official documents, and historical records. No other written languages based on regional dialects have had comparable status. There is, therefore, continuity from the earliest written forms of Chinese to the Chinese of the present day. The script of the written language, which is not phonetic (that is, a Chinese character provides no clue to its pronunciation), also gives the impression that the Chinese language is uniform, since the same script is used for ancient classical texts as well as for modern prose. Today, an educated Chinese speaker can freely use expressions of classical Chinese and modern-day expressions in the same dialog without feeling that he or she is switching between two languages.

Spoken Chinese is different. A large number of regional dialects have developed across China. At the present time, there are seven dialect groups, and each group includes many dialects. Although local varieties are referred to as "dialects," they are, in fact, different languages, because their speakers can hardly understand each other. For example, a speaker of the Shanghai dialect cannot understand a speaker of Cantonese, even though the two can communicate with each other by means of the written script, which is independent of sounds. Standard Chinese, the variety of Chinese taught in school, is based on the Beijing dialect, itself a member of Mandarin, a dialect family spoken in northern and southwestern China.

Modern Chinese contains a significant amount of classical Chinese, especially in the written language. Knowledge of classical Chinese is admired among Chinese speakers. It is not uncommon to find children as young as six years old who have memorized poems written in the Tang dynasty (618–907 CE). In school, students read texts in classical Chinese. The influence of classical Chinese can be seen in the words that are used, as well as in the structure of a sentence. For example, there is often more than one way to describe an object or a concept, both in the spoken style and the classical, written style. Compare the following.

SPOKEN LANGUAGE		WRITTEN LANGUAGE		ENGLISH MEANING
喜欢	xǐhuan	爱好	àihào	to like
吃饭	chīfàn	进食	jìnshí	to eat a meal
站	zhàn	立	lì	to stand
一些	yìxiē	若干	ruògān	some
要是	yàoshi	倘若	tǎngruò	if
马上	mǎshàng	立即	lìjí	immediately

As you make progress in Chinese, you will encounter more and more expressions that come from classical Chinese.

Parts of speech

Introducing the parts of speech

Both English and Chinese words are categorized by parts of speech. You may have learned these in elementary school without understanding their usefulness. They are important, because different rules apply to the different categories. In your own language, you do this naturally, unless the word is new to you. You know to say *one horse, two horses*, adding an *-s* to make the noun *horse* plural. You do not try to apply a noun's rule to a verb and say *I am, we ams*; instead, you say *we are*. People learning a foreign language sometimes use the wrong set of rules, however, because all of the forms are new, so nothing "sounds wrong." To avoid this kind of mistake, learn the part of speech when you learn a new vocabulary word.

Parts of speech help you identify words, so that even if a word is used in several ways (and this happens in both English and Chinese), you can determine the Chinese equivalent. For instance, 那 *nà* "that" can be

1. a demonstrative adjective

    那个人没法儿跟他讲道理。
    Nà ge rén méi fǎr gēn tā jiǎng dàolǐ.
    That man is impossible. (LITERALLY,
        That man, we can't reason with him.)

2. a pronoun

    那个我不知道。
    Nà ge wǒ bù zhīdào.
    I don't know **that**. (LITERALLY, **That** I don't
        know.)

3. an adverbial conjunction

    那我等一下再来。
    Nà wǒ děngyíxià zài lái.
    In that case, I will come a bit later.

When you know the parts of speech, the fact that a word is used several ways in English won't cause you to choose the wrong one in Chinese.

Following is a list of the parts of speech. The parts are described (1) in traditional definitions, (2) by the forms that identify them, and (3) by their functions (as structural linguists think of them).

Nouns

1. Names or words standing for persons, places, things, or abstract concepts

    John
    man
    Beijing
    city
    table
    justice

2. Words that become plural by adding *-s* or *-es* (in addition to a few other ways)

    book ~ books
    fox ~ foxes
    child ~ children

3. Words that function as subjects, objects, or complements

    John *is here.*
    She read the **book**.
    There is **Mary**.

Pronouns

1. Words that substitute for nouns

    John is already here. Have you seen **him**?

2. Words that are used when no noun is identified

    It *is raining.*
    They *say . . .*
    You *never know.*

3. Words that serve the same function as nouns

    He *is here.*
    He *loves* **her**.
    There **it** *is.*

Adjectives

1. Words that modify, limit, or qualify a noun or pronoun

    dumb
    red
    serious
    happy

2. Words that may be inflected (may change form) or may be preceded by *more* or *most* to make comparisons

    dumb ~ dumber ~ dumbest
    *serious ~ **more** serious ~ **most** serious*

Adverbs

1. Words that modify verbs, adjectives, or other adverbs by telling how, when, where, or how much

    *We'll come **soon**.*
    *It's **really** big.*
    *They do it **very** well.*

2. Words that can show comparison between verbs (as adjectives do for nouns)

    soon ~ sooner ~ soonest
    *rapidly ~ **more** rapidly ~ **most** rapidly*

Conjunctions

1. Coordinating conjunctions (for example, *and, but,* and *so*) connect words, phrases, or clauses that are grammatically equivalent.

    *John **and** Mary*
    *on the table, **but** under a napkin*
    *I had no money, **so** I stayed at home.*

2. Subordinating conjunctions (for example, *if, because,* and *when*) connect subordinate clauses to the main clause of a sentence.

    ***When** you see it, you will believe me.*

Interjections

1. Exclamations

    Hey!
    Wow!

2. Words that can be used alone or in sentences

    Darn!
    ***Oh,** Mary, is it true?*

Prepositions

1. Words that express place, time, and other circumstances and show the relationship between two elements in a sentence

    at
    for
    in
    of
    on
    to

2. Words that are not inflected (never change form)

3. Words that have a noun or pronoun as their object

    ***in** a minute*
    ***of** a sort*
    ***on** it*

These groups are called prepositional phrases.

Verbs

1. Words that express action, existence, or state of being

    speak
    learn
    run
    be
    have
    feel

2. Words that may be inflected to show person (*I **am** ~ he **is***), time (*I **sing** ~ I **sang***), voice (*I **write** ~ it **is written***), and mood (*if I **am** here ~ if I **were** you*)

3

Nouns

Definition See page 6.

Forms English nouns are considered to have gender, number, and case.

GENDER Masculine or feminine gender is used only for someone or something that is male or female.

> *man*
> *woman*
> *bull*
> *tigress*

All other nouns are neuter. Gender makes no difference in English except when there are two forms for one noun (for example, *actor* and *actress*) or when the nouns are replaced by pronouns (for example, *he, she, it*).

NUMBER Most nouns add *-s* or *-es* to the singular form to form the plural.

> *train ~ trains*
> *box ~ boxes*

Some nouns have irregular plural forms.

> *mouse ~ mice*
> *man ~ men*
> *child ~ children*

CASE There is only one extra case in English: the possessive, or genitive. It is formed by adding *-'s* to a singular noun or *-'* to a plural noun ending in *-s*.

> **Mary's** *book*
> *the* **book's** *cover*
> *the* **books'** *covers*

The possessive case can often be ignored, and *of* used instead, although this form is less common when a person is involved.

> *Kant's theories → the theories* **of Kant**
> *the book's pages → the pages* **of the book**

Nouns are often preceded by determiners (see page 16).

> **a** *book,* **the** *book,* **my** *book,* **two** *books*

Uses The three most common uses of nouns are as subjects, objects, and complements (see page 14).

SUBJECT	**Mrs. Li** *is Chinese.*
APPOSITIVE	*Mrs. Li, a Chinese* **woman**, *is visiting us.*
DIRECT OBJECT OF A VERB	*He has a* **pencil**.
INDIRECT OBJECT OF A VERB	*She gave the hat to* **Paul**.
OBJECT OF A PREPOSITION	*We are in the* **room**.
COMPLEMENT	*It is a valuable* **book**.
ADJECTIVE	*I have my* **history** *textbook.*

CONTINUED ON PAGE 12 ▶

Chinese Introducing nouns

Definition See page 6.

Forms GENDER Chinese nouns do not have gender.

NUMBER Most Chinese nouns do not have number; however, certain nouns referring to people have a form for more than one.

朋友 *péngyou* friend   朋友们 *péngyǒumen* friends
老师 *lǎoshī* teacher   老师们 *lǎoshīmen* teachers

REDUPLICATION A common type of Chinese noun is formed by reduplication. For example, nouns referring to family members are formed in this way.

爸爸 *bàba* father   妈妈 *māma* mother
哥哥 *gēge* older brother   姐姐 *jiějie* older sister
弟弟 *dìdi* younger brother   妹妹 *mèimei* younger sister

CASE Chinese nouns do not have case.

Chinese nouns are often preceded by determiners (see page 17).

一本书 *yì běn shū* one book
这本书 *zhè běn shū* this book
那些书 *nà xiē shū* those books

Uses Chinese nouns are used in the same way as English nouns. Compare the following sentences with the English examples on the opposite page.

SUBJECT	李太太是中国人。 **Lǐ tàitai** shì Zhōngguó rén. **Mrs. Li** is Chinese.
APPOSITIVE	李太太，一位中国**女士**，来拜访我们。 Lǐ tàitai, yí wèi Zhōngguó **nǚshì**, lái bàifǎng wǒmen. Mrs. Li, a Chinese **woman**, came to visit us.
DIRECT OBJECT OF A VERB	他有一支**铅笔**。 Tā yǒu yì zhī **qiānbǐ**. He has a **pencil**.
INDIRECT OBJECT OF A VERB	她送了一顶帽子给**小明**。 Tā song le yì dǐng màozi gěi **Xiǎomíng**. She gave a hat to **Xiaoming**.
OBJECT OF A PREPOSITION	我们坐在**门口**。 Wǒmen zuò zài **ménkǒu**. We are sitting at the **doorway**.
COMPLEMENT	这是一本有价值的**书**。 Zhè shì yì běn yǒu jiàzhí de **shū**. This is a valuable **book**.
ADJECTIVE	我有**历史**书。 Wǒ yǒu **lìshǐ** shū. I have **history** books.

CONTINUED ON PAGE 13 ▶

Types   There are several ways to classify nouns. Following are two important ones.

1. Common vs. proper

   Common nouns are applied to a class of individuals. They begin with a lowercase letter.

   > *student*
   > *country*
   > *cat*
   > *language*

   Proper nouns name a specific individual within a class. They begin with a capital letter.

   > *Miss Jones*
   > *China*
   > *Kitty*
   > *English*

2. Countable vs. mass

   Countable nouns can be counted.

   > *one pencil*
   > *two sharks*
   > *three engineers*

   Mass nouns cannot be separated into individuals—they cannot be counted.

   > *salt*
   > *weather*
   > *sadness*

Types   Chinese nouns may be classified as follows.

1. Common vs. proper

   Common nouns in Chinese are generally the same as their English counterparts, but **proper nouns** referring to people differ from those in English in that the last name precedes a title.

   李太太 *Lǐ tàitai*   Mrs. Li

2. Countable vs. mass

   Countable nouns in Chinese differ from those in English in a major way: they usually need to be accompanied by a **measure word** (see Appendix A, page 145).

   一个人 *yí **ge** rén*   a MW person

   A measure word (indicated by MW in the English translations of examples) indicates the quantity or a permanent quality of the noun that follows.

Introducing subjects and objects

Subjects

Subjects are most frequently nouns or pronouns. The subject of a verb is the person or thing that *is* something or *is doing* something.

> ***Mary*** and ***I*** are here.
> ***John*** speaks Chinese.
> Are ***they*** (the textbooks) *arriving today?*

 QUICK CHECK

Ask yourself: *Who* is here? *Who* speaks Chinese? *What* is arriving?

Answer: the subject

In normal word order, the subject comes before the verb. The subject is usually, but not always, the first word in a sentence or clause.

Subject complements

Subject complements are words or phrases that define, or complete an idea about, the subject.

> Mr. White is a ***professor***.
> *Jeanne and Alice are* ***Americans***.

Direct objects

Some systems of grammar refer to direct objects as "object complements." The name matters less than the ability to recognize their important function. Direct objects are usually nouns or pronouns that directly receive the verb's action. In normal word order, the direct object comes after the verb.

> *Mary likes* ***John***. *She likes* ***him***.
> *The professor is giving a* ***test***. *He is giving* ***it***.

☑ QUICK CHECK

Ask yourself: *Who* is liked? *What* is being given?

Answer: the direct object

Indirect objects

Indirect objects are usually nouns or pronouns that are indirectly affected by the verb's action. They indicate *to* whom or *for* whom something is done.

> *Speak* ***to me****!*

Verbs of communication often have implied direct objects, as in *Tell me (the news)*. These objects are sometimes expressed in other languages.

COMBINATIONS Some verbs (for example, *give, tell,* and *buy*) can have more than one object. In addition to a direct object, there can be an indirect object. Counting the subject, there can be three nouns or pronouns with different functions, even in a short sentence.

> ***Robert*** *gives* ***the book*** **to Alice**.
> SUBJECT   DIRECT OBJECT   INDIRECT OBJECT

> ***Robert*** *gives* ***Alice*** **the book**.
> SUBJECT   INDIRECT OBJECT   DIRECT OBJECT

> ***He*** *gives* ***it*** **to her**.
> SUBJECT   DIRECT OBJECT   INDIRECT OBJECT

Notice that the two possible word orders have no effect on which object is direct and which is indirect. The word order in English simply determines whether or not the word *to* is used.

☑ QUICK CHECK

To analyze the sentences above, ask yourself: *Who gives?*

Answer: *Robert* or *he* (the subject)

Who or *what* is given?

Answer: *the book* or *it* (the direct object)

To/for whom / to/for what is it given?

Answer: *Alice* or *her* (the indirect object)

Objects of prepositions

All prepositions must have objects (see page 7). These objects immediately follow the preposition.

*on the **table*** ~ *on **it***
*after **Peter*** ~ *after **him***

In questions and relative clauses in English (see page 76), this rule is often ignored, and the preposition is used alone at the end of the sentence.

***To whom** did you give it?*
→ ***Whom** did you give it **to**?*

English Introducing determiners

Definition   Determiners are words that introduce nouns and their adjectives. They usually come first in a noun phrase.

>*the* red book
>*a* tall boy
>*each* window
>*several* students

Types   Many kinds of words can serve as determiners: definite articles, indefinite articles, partitives, numbers, and general words like *each, either,* and *several.* Some types of adjectives (possessives, demonstratives, and interrogatives) can also be determiners; these are discussed in Chapter 5.

Forms   The **definite article** is always written *the,* but it is pronounced like *thee* before words beginning with a vowel or silent *h* (*the book* vs. *the apple, the hour*). The **indefinite article** is *a* or *an* in the singular, *some* in the plural. *An* is used before words beginning with a vowel or silent *h.* Other forms of determiners do not change their spelling or pronunciation.

Uses   DEFINITE ARTICLES *The* indicates a specific noun.

>*The* book (the one you wanted) *is on the table.*

INDEFINITE ARTICLES *A/an* refers to any individual in a class.

>I see *a* boy (not a specific one).

OTHER DETERMINERS The use of other determiners is governed by their meaning.

>*some* boys
>*few* boys
>*several* boys
>*eight* boys

Types   Chinese does not have definite articles or indefinite articles. To refer to specific nouns, demonstrative pronouns (see page 37) are used. To refer to any member of a class, the numeral 一 *yī* "one" followed by a measure word (for example, 个 *ge*) is used.

> 一个学生 *yí ge xuésheng* a student

Chinese determiners include words and phrases that refer to quantity, such as 很多 *hěn duō* "many," 几个 *jǐ ge* "a few MW," 每个 and *měi ge* "each MW." Demonstrative pronouns can also be part of a determiner (see page 37).

Forms   A measure word may or may not be included as part of a determiner.

1. Measure word included

   Numeral + measure word ("MW")

   > 三辆车 *sān liàng chē* three cars
   > 五只猫 *wǔ zhī māo* five cats

   几 *jǐ* + measure word ("a few MW")

   > 几本书 *jǐ běn shū* a few books
   > 几个人 *jǐ ge rén* a few people

   每 *měi* + measure word ("each/every MW")

   > 每个老师 *měi ge lǎoshī* each/every teacher
   > 每棵树 *měi kē shù* each/every tree

2. Measure word not included

   一些 *yì xiē* ("some")

   > 一些人 *yì xiē rén* some people
   > 一些水 *yì xiē shuǐ* some water

   很多 *hěn duō* ("much/many")

   > 很多故事 *hěn duō gùshi* many stories
   > 很多茶 *hěn duō chá* a lot of tea

Uses   To specify quantity, the exact amount or number is indicated by a numeral.

> ☑ QUICK CHECK

NUMERAL	+ MEASURE WORD	+ NOUN	ENGLISH MEANING
一 *yí*	个 *ge*	小孩 *xiǎohái*	a child
两 *liáng*	张 *zhāng*	照片 *zhàopiàn*	two pictures
三 *sān*	只 *zhī*	狗 *gǒu*	three dogs

NOTE In spoken Chinese, the word 两 *liǎng* is normally used for the numeral 2 instead of 二 *èr*.

Pronouns

English Introducing pronouns

Definition   See page 6.

Forms   Like nouns, English pronouns have gender, number, and case, but further distinctions can be made. They also show person.

PERSON English distinguishes three persons. **First person** is the one who is speaking (*I, me, we, us*). **Second person** is the one being spoken to (*you*). **Third person** is the one being spoken about (*he, him, she, her, it, they, them*). Both pronouns and verbs are listed according to person.

GENDER Some, but not all, pronouns can be distinguished by gender. *I* can refer to either a man or a woman. *She*, however, is always feminine, *he* is always masculine, and *it*, even if it refers to an animal, is always neuter.

NUMBER Each of the three persons may be either singular or plural.

CASE Pronouns show more cases than nouns: the subjective (for example, *I* and *she*), the possessive (for example, *my/mine* and *her/hers*), and the objective (*me* and *her*). These are discussed below, under Uses.

Uses   Personal pronouns have the same functions as nouns.

1. Subject

    She *is here.*

2. Direct object

    *I like **them**.*

3. Indirect object

    *I am giving **him** the book.*

4. Object of a preposition

    *The question is hard for **me**.*

5. Complement

    *It is **she** who is speaking.*

Types   There are several types of pronouns.

1. Personal (page 22)

2. Possessive (page 24)

3. Reflexive/reciprocal (page 26)

4. Disjunctive (page 28)

5. Relative (page 30)

6. Demonstrative (page 36)

7. Interrogative (page 38)

Chinese Introducing pronouns

Definitions and uses of pronouns are generally the same in Chinese as in English. However, there are three important differences.

1. Chinese personal pronouns do not have case, and they have gender only in the third person. They do, however, show person and number.

2. The personal pronoun for "you" has two forms: the regular forms 你 *nǐ* (singular) and 你们 *nǐmen* (plural), and the honorific 您 *nín* (used for both the singular and plural). 您 *nín* is used to show respect for teachers, guests, and elders.

3. Chinese does not have relative pronouns. Relative clauses are formed with the particle 的 *de* (see page 31).

English Personal pronouns

Subject pronouns (see page 14)

	SINGULAR	PLURAL
FIRST PERSON	*I*	*we*
SECOND PERSON	*you*	*you*
THIRD PERSON	*he, she, it, one* (indefinite)	*they*

John gives a present. → *He gives it.* (third-person singular)
Mary and I arrive. → *We arrive.* (first-person plural)

Direct object pronouns (see page 14)

	SINGULAR	PLURAL
FIRST PERSON	*me*	*us*
SECOND PERSON	*you*	*you*
THIRD PERSON	*him, her, it, one*	*them*

*He sees **me**, and I see **you**.*
*You will find **them**.*

Indirect object pronouns (see page 14)

	SINGULAR	PLURAL
FIRST PERSON	*(to/for) me*	*(to/for) us*
SECOND PERSON	*(to/for) you*	*(to/for) you*
THIRD PERSON	*(to/for) him, her, it, one*	*(to/for) them*

*They send the letter **to us**.*
*He writes **her** a letter.*
*I bought a dress **for her**.*
*I got **them** a ticket.*

Objects of prepositions (see page 15)

After a preposition, English uses the same form of the pronoun as for direct objects.

Be careful with compound pronoun subjects or objects. These remain in the same case as that for a single subject or object.

> *I am Chinese. **She** and **I** are Chinese.*
> *This is between **us**. This is between **you** and **me**.*
> *Give it to **them**. Give it to **him** and **her**.*

WORD ORDER When there are two pronoun objects in English, the direct object comes before the indirect object.

> *He shows **it** to **them**.*

When a noun and a pronoun are used together, word order can vary.

He shows	***the book***	***to them****.*
	DIRECT OBJECT	INDIRECT OBJECT

He shows	***them***	***the book****.*
	INDIRECT OBJECT	DIRECT OBJECT

chinese Personal pronouns

Chinese makes no distinction between subject pronouns, direct object pronouns, indirect object pronouns, and pronouns that function as objects of prepositions. The same forms express all four uses.

	SINGULAR	PLURAL
FIRST PERSON	我 *wǒ*	我们 *wǒmen*
SECOND PERSON	你 *nǐ*	你们 *nǐmen*
	您 *nín*	您 *nín*
THIRD PERSON	他 *tā* (masc.)	他们 *tāmen* (masc.)
	她 *tā* (fem.)	她们 *tāmen* (fem.)
	它 *tā* (inanimate)	它们 *tāmen* (inanimate)

您 is the respectful form for the second person; its singular and plural forms are the same. In the singular and plural of the third person, the masculine, feminine, and inanimate forms have the same sounds; they differ only in written form.

Subject pronouns

小王和我是学生。 → 我们是学生。
Xiǎo Wáng hé wǒ shì xuésheng. **Wǒmen** *shì xuésheng.*
Xiao Wang and I are students. **We** are students.

李明写完了作业。 → 他写完了。
Lǐ Míng xiě wán le zuòyè. **Tā** *xiě wán le 0.*
Li Míng finished the homework. **He** finished (it).

The third-person inanimate pronoun is usually not expressed when it functions as an object; it is understood from the context.

Object pronouns

他看见**我**，我看见**你**。
*Tā kànjiàn **wǒ**, wǒ kànjiàn **nǐ**.*
He sees **me**, and I see **you**.

你会找到**他们**。
*Nǐ huì zhǎodào **tāmen**.*
You will find **them**.

Indirect object pronouns

他们把信寄给**我们**。
*Tāmen bǎ xìn jì gěi **wǒmen**.*
They send the letter to **us**.

他给**她**写了一封信。
*Tā gěi **tā** xiě le yì fēng xìn.*
He wrote **her** a letter.

Objects of prepositions

她对**我们**很亲切。
*Tā duì **wǒmen** hěn qīnqiè.*
She is very friendly to **us**.

我想跟**他**一块儿去看电影。
*Wǒ xiǎng gēn **tā** yíkuàir qù kàn diànyǐng.*
I would like to go to the movies with **him**.

Definition A possessive pronoun replaces a possessive adjective (or a noun in the possessive) plus a noun.

> It's **my book**. → It's **mine**.
> It's **Anne's car**. → It's **hers**.

Forms Possessive pronouns have person and number; in the third-person singular, they also have gender. They do not have case, that is, they have the same form no matter what function they perform in a sentence.

	SINGULAR	PLURAL
FIRST PERSON	*mine*	*ours*
SECOND PERSON	*yours*	*yours*
THIRD PERSON	*his, hers, its, one's*	*theirs*

If you know the person, gender, and number of the possessor (*Mary* in the example below), there is only one choice for the pronoun (in this example, *hers*).

> *You have your book; where is* **Mary's** *book (***her*** book)?*

To avoid repeating *book,* it is replaced along with the possessive noun or adjective in front of it. Since *Mary's* (or *her*) is third-person singular feminine, *hers* is the correct pronoun.

> *You have your book; where is* **hers**?

Pronominal possessive forms

Forms   Chinese does not have possessive pronouns. To express possession, the combination of a
personal pronoun and the particle 的 *de* is used.

	SINGULAR PRONOUN + 的 *de*	PLURAL PRONOUN + 的 *de*
FIRST PERSON	我的 *wǒ de*	我们的 *wǒmen de*
SECOND PERSON	你的 *nǐ de*	你们的 *nǐmen de*
	您的 *nín de*	您的 *nín de*
THIRD PERSON	他的 *tā de* (masc.)	他们的 *tāmen de* (masc.)
	她的 *tā de* (fem.)	她们的 *tāmen de* (fem.)
	它的 *tā de* (inanimate)	它们的 *tāmen de* (inanimate)

这是我的书。   → 这是**我的**。
Zhè shì wǒ de shū.   *Zhè shì **wǒ de**.*
This is my book.   This is **mine**.

我的书在这儿，你的书呢？   → 我的书在这儿，**你的**呢？
Wǒ de shū zài zhèr, nǐ de shū ne?   *Wǒ de shū zài zhèr, **nǐ de** ne?*
My book is here; where is your book?   My book is here; where is **yours**?

English   Reflexive/reciprocal pronouns

Definition Reflexive pronouns are pronoun objects or complements that refer to the same person(s) or thing(s) as another element in the sentence, usually the subject.

Forms

	SINGULAR	PLURAL	RECIPROCAL
FIRST PERSON	*myself*	*ourselves*	*each other/one another*
SECOND PERSON	*yourself*	*yourselves*	*each other/one another*
THIRD PERSON	*himself, herself, itself, oneself*	*themselves*	*each other/one another*

Uses Reflexive pronouns are used as objects of verbs and prepositions.

Types A reflexive pronoun is normally used only when the subject acts directly on himself/herself or does something for himself/herself directly.

> **Paul** cut **himself**.
> **I** told **myself** it didn't matter.

Occasionally, reflexive pronouns are used idiomatically.

> **They** always enjoy **themselves**.

For mutual or reciprocal action, *each other* or *one another* is used. This expression does not change form.

> **They** congratulated **each other**.
> **You** two saw **each other** last night.

Reflexive/reciprocal pronouns can function as direct or indirect object pronouns.

> **They** saw **each other**.
> **We** talked to **each other** yesterday.

In English, reflexive and reciprocal objects are often omitted.

> **We talked** yesterday. (*To each other* is understood.)

Sometimes, a construction is used that requires no object.

> **Paul got hurt**. (*Hurt himself* is understood.)

However, consider the following sentence.

> *We washed this morning.*

If you have not heard the rest of the conversation, the meaning is ambiguous. The sentence may have either of the following meanings.

> *We washed ourselves (got washed).*
> *We washed our clothes (did the laundry).*

Chinese Reflexive/reciprocal forms

Forms The short form for "self," 自己 *zìjǐ*, does not change, regardless of person or number.

The long form combines the personal pronoun and the reflexive short form.

	SINGULAR	PLURAL
FIRST PERSON	我自己 *wǒ zìjǐ*	我们自己 *wǒmen zìjǐ*
SECOND PERSON	你自己 *nǐ zìjǐ*	你们自己 *nǐmen zìjǐ*
	您自己 *nín zìjǐ*	您自己 *nín zìjǐ*
THIRD PERSON	他自己 *tā zìjǐ*	他们自己 *tāmen zìjǐ*
	她自己 *tā zìjǐ*	她们自己 *tāmen zìjǐ*
	它自己 *tā zìjǐ*	它们自己 *tāmen zìjǐ*

Chinese does not have reciprocal pronouns. For mutual or reciprocal action, the adverb 互相 *hùxiāng* "mutually" is used.

他们常互相批评。
Tāmen cháng hùxiāng pīpíng.
They often criticize each other.

Uses The short and long forms for "self" are used as objects of verbs and prepositions.

SHORT FORM	LONG FORM
他常批评自己。	他常批评他自己。
*Tā cháng pīpíng **zìjǐ**.*	*Tā cháng pīpíng **tā zìjǐ**.*
He often criticizes **himself**.	**He** often criticizes **himself**.
我跟自己说话。	我跟我自己说话。
*Wǒ gēn **zìjǐ** shuōhuà.*	*Wǒ gēn **wǒ zìjǐ** shuōhuà.*
I talk to **myself**.	I talk to **myself**.

English Disjunctive pronouns

Definition   A disjunctive pronoun is not attached to a verb. (*Disjunctive* means "not joined.") It is used alone or as an extra word to give special emphasis or to intensify an impression.

Forms and uses   The form of a disjunctive pronoun depends on its use.

1. Used alone, the disjunctive pronoun is in the subjective case (if required) in formal English, and in the objective case for informal use.

   Who's there?   **I**. (formal; *I am* is understood)
   Me. (informal)

2. As an intensifier, the reflexive pronoun is normally used.

   I'll do it **myself**!
   He told me so **himself**.

3. Sometimes, we merely raise our voices for emphasis.

   You *do it!*

Chinese Disjunctive pronouns

Forms The forms of these pronouns depend on their use.

Uses Disjunctive pronouns may be used in the following ways.

1. Alone

谁在那儿?　　**我**。
Shéi zài nàr?　　***Wǒ***.
Who's there?　　**I/Me**.

2. As an intensifier (the short form of the reflexive pronoun is typically used)

我自己做!
*Wǒ **zìjǐ** zuò!*
I'll do it **myself**!

他自己告诉我的。
*Tā **zìjǐ** gàosu wǒ de.*
He told me so **himself**.

3. After a preposition (see page 77)

这一切都是因为**你**。
*Zhè yíqiè dōu shì yīnwèi **nǐ**.*
This is all because of **you**.

English Relative pronouns

Definition   Relative pronouns begin a relative clause. They refer to a noun, called the antecedent, and usually come directly after that noun.

Forms   Relative pronouns have the following forms in English.

	SUBJECT	OBJECT	POSSESSIVE	INDIRECT OBJECT/PREPOSITIONAL OBJECT
PERSON	*who/that*	*whom/that*	*whose*	*to/by whom*
THING	*which/that*	*which/that*	*whose/*	*to/by which*
			of which	*where* (for place prepositions)
				when (for time prepositions)

The correct pronoun is determined by the following factors.

1. Whether the antecedent is a person or a thing

2. The function of the pronoun in the clause

3. For subjects and objects, whether the clause is restrictive or nonrestrictive

   A **restrictive clause** defines the noun. *That* is used, and the clause is not set off by commas.

   > The book **that** *you just read is world-renowned.*

   Without the clause, you would not know which book is meant. It is an essential definition.

   A **nonrestrictive clause** describes the noun, rather than defines it. It is not necessary to form a complete sentence. *Who, whom,* or *which* is used, and the clause is set off by commas.

   > Dream of the Red Chamber, **which** *the class is going to read, is famous.*

   The relative clause could be eliminated, and the sentence would still make sense. It is a nonessential description.

Uses   Relative pronouns have several uses.

1. They introduce clauses that give additional information about the antecedent.

2. They allow you to join two short sentences to make your writing smoother and to avoid repetition.

   > *Mrs. Li came yesterday. Mrs. Li is an expert pianist.*
   > → *Mrs. Li,* **who** *is an expert pianist, came yesterday.*

3. They can be subjects, direct objects, indirect objects, possessives, or objects of a preposition in the relative clause.

4. They are inflected only for case, not for person or number. Their form depends on their function in the clause.

   The function of the antecedent in the main clause has no effect on the form of the relative pronoun.

Chinese Relative clauses

Forms Unlike English, Chinese has no relative pronouns. Instead, the particle 的 *de* is used to connect the relative clause with the noun it refers to.

Uses In English, the relative clause occurs after the noun it modifies, while in Chinese the relative clause occurs before the noun.

Either the subject or the object is not expressed in the relative clause. The relative clause is immediately followed by the particle 的 *de*, which is then followed by the noun that the clause refers to.

1. Subject not expressed

   [昨天来]　　 的　那　个　人　　 是　我叔叔。
   [***Zuótiān lái***]　***de*** *nà*　*ge*　*rén*　　*shì*　*wǒ shūshu*。
   yesterday came　*de*　that　MW　person　is　my uncle
   The man **who came yesterday** is my uncle.

2. Object not expressed

   [你买]　　 的　那　本　书　　 很有名。
   [***Nǐ mǎi***]　***de***　*nà*　*běn*　*shū*　　*hěn yǒumíng*
   you bought　*de*　that　MW　book　very well-known
   The book **that you bought** is very well-known.

English How to analyze relative clauses

Mr. Smith *is **an excellent cook**.*
SUBJECT   COMPLEMENT

Mr. Smith *made **these pies**.*
SUBJECT   DIRECT OBJECT

1. Find the repeated element. → *Mr. Smith*
2. Identify the function of the repeated element in the second sentence, which will become the relative clause. → the subject
3. Choose the relative pronoun. → *who* (person, subject)
4. Copy the first sentence through the antecedent. → *Mr. Smith . . .*
5. Put in the correct relative pronoun, in this case, *who.* → *Mr. Smith, who . . .*
6. Copy the rest of the second sentence (now a relative clause). → *Mr. Smith, who made these pies . . .*
7. Copy the rest of the first sentence. → *Mr. Smith, who made these pies, is an excellent cook.*

Other examples follow.

The ten books are on the table. I am reading them.
*The ten books **that I am reading** are on the table.*

> *That* is used because it
>
> 1. is the object of *am reading* in the clause (no commas).
> 2. refers to a thing.
> 3. is restrictive (defines which ten books).

Mr. Jones died today. I saw him yesterday.
*Mr. Jones, **whom I saw yesterday**, died today.*

> *Whom* is used because it
>
> 1. is the object of *I saw* (with commas).
> 2. refers to a person.
> 3. is nonrestrictive. (You already know who Mr. Jones is. This merely gives an extra fact about him.)

The student is asleep. I am speaking to that student.
*The student **to whom I am speaking** is asleep.*

> *To whom* is used because it
>
> 1. is the indirect object (no commas).
> 2. refers to a person.
> 3. is restrictive (defines which student).

CONTINUED ON PAGE 34 ▶

张先生是一位优秀的厨师。
Zhāng xiānsheng *shì yí wèi yōuxiù de* ***chúshī***.
SUBJECT   COMPLEMENT
Mr. Zhang is an excellent cook.

张先生做了这些春卷。
Zhāng xiānsheng *zuò le zhè xiē* ***chūnjuǎn***.
SUBJECT   DIRECT OBJECT
Mr. Zhang made these egg rolls.

There are two things to consider: the function of the repeated element and the word order.

1. Find the repeated element. → 张先生 *Zhāng xiānsheng* "Mr. Zhang"

2. Identify the function of the repeated element in the second sentence, which will become the relative clause. → the subject

3. Copy the second sentence. → 张先生做了这些春卷 *Zhāng xiānsheng zuò le zhè xiē chūnjuǎn*.

4. Delete the subject (the repeated element) from the copied sentence; this becomes the relative clause. → 做了这些春卷 *Zuò le zhèxiē chūnjuǎn*.

5. Add the particle 的 *de* after the relative clause. → 做了这些春卷的 *Zuò le zhè xiē chūnjuǎn de*

6. Copy the first sentence, placing it after the relative clause with 的. → 做了这些春卷的张先生是一位优秀的厨师 *Zuò le zhè xiē chūnjuǎn de Zhāng xiānsheng shì yí wèi yōuxiù de chúshī*. Mr. Zhang, who made these egg rolls, is an excellent cook.

Try this with other sentences. Follow the same steps until they feel natural.

那三本书在桌上。   我正在看那三本书。
Nà sān běn shū *zài zhuōshang*.   *Wǒ zhèngzài kàn* ***nà sān běn shū***.
The three books are on the table.   I'm reading **those three books**.

→ 我正在看的那三本书在桌上。
Wǒ zhèngzài kàn de nà sān běn shū zài zhuōshang.
The three books **that I'm reading** are on the table.

王先生今天去世了。   我昨天看见王先生。
Wáng xiānsheng *jīntiān qùshì le*.   *Wǒ zuótiān kànjiàn* ***Wáng xiānsheng***.
Mr. Wang died today.   I saw **Mr. Wang** yesterday.

→ 我昨天看见的王先生今天去世了。
Wǒ zuótiān kànjiàn de *Wáng xiānsheng jīntiān qùshì le*.
Mr. Wang, **whom I saw yesterday**, died today.

If the repeated element, which may be a noun or a pronoun, functions as the object of a preposition in the relative clause, it is not deleted but is kept in the form of a pronoun.

那个学生在睡觉。   我在跟他说话。
Nà ge xuésheng *zài shuìjiào*.   *Wǒ zài* ***gēn tā*** *shuōhuà*.
That student is asleep.   I'm speaking **to him**.

→ 我在跟他说话的那个学生在睡觉。
Wǒ zài gēn tā shuōhuà de *nà ge xuésheng zài shuìjiào*.
The student **whom I'm speaking to** is asleep.

CONTINUED ON PAGE 35 ▶

The old house is falling down. I lived in that house as a child.
*The old house **where** (**in which**) **I lived as a child** is falling down.*

Where is used because it

1. replaces a place preposition plus noun object (no commas).
2. refers to a thing. (*In which* is also correct.)

The woman lives in New York. I took her coat.
*The woman **whose coat I took** lives in New York.*

Whose is used because it

1. is possessive (no commas).
2. refers to a person.
3. is restrictive (defines which woman).

If the repeated element indicates a location, the entire location phrase, including the preposition 在 *zài* "at" and the location particle 里 *li* "in," is deleted.

那个老房子快要倒了。 我小时候住在那个老房子里。
Nà ge lǎo fángzi kuàiyào dǎo le. *Wǒ xiǎo shíhou zhù zài nà ge lǎo fángzi li.*
That old house is falling down. I lived **in that old house** as a child.

→ 我小时候住的那个老房子快要倒了。
Wǒ xiǎo shíhou zhù de nà ge lǎo fángzi kuàiyào dǎo le.
That old house **where (in which) I lived as a child** is falling down.

If the repeated element is a possessive pronoun, it is not deleted.

那位女士住在纽约。 我拿了她的上衣。
Nà wèi nǚshì zhù zài Niǔyuē. *Wǒ ná le tā de shàngyī.*
That woman lives in New York. I took **her** coat.

→ 我拿了她的上衣的那位女士住在纽约。
Wǒ ná le tā de shàngyī de nà wèi nǚshì zhù zài Niǔyuē.
That woman **whose coat I took** lives in New York.

English Demonstrative pronouns

Definition Demonstrative pronouns point out someone or something.

Forms There are four forms of the demonstrative pronoun in English.

SINGULAR	PLURAL
this (one)	*these*
that (one)	*those*

Uses These pronouns distinguish only between what is near (*this, these*) and far (*that, those*) and between singular and plural. No changes are made for gender or case.

I can't decide which of the chairs to buy.
__This one__ is lovely, but __that one__ is comfortable.
__This__ is lovely, but __that__ is comfortable.

Chinese Demonstrative pronouns

Forms Demonstrative pronouns distinguish between what is near and what is far, and between singular and plural. There are two plural forms in Chinese, depending on whether a numeral is expressed or not.

	SINGULAR	PLURAL	PLURAL WITH NUMERAL
NEAR	这 *zhè* MW this	这些 *zhè xiē* these	这 *zhè* [NUMERAL] MW these [NUMERAL]
FAR	那 *nà* MW that	那些 *nà xiē* those	那 *nà* [NUMERAL] MW those [NUMERAL]

Uses A demonstrative pronoun is used to replace a noun or a noun phrase that functions as the subject or object of a verb.

Singular forms are almost always followed by a measure word.

> 我不能决定买哪一个电脑。
> *Wǒ bùnéng juédìng mǎi nǎ yí ge diànnǎo.*
> I can't decide which of the computers to buy.

> 这个很轻；那个很漂亮。
> *Zhè ge hěn qīng, nà ge hěn piàoliang.*
> **This one** is light; **that one** is pretty.

The only time that a singular form is used alone, without a measure word, is in a question of identification.

> 这是什么？
> *Zhè shì shénme?*
> What is **this**?

There are two plural forms of the demonstrative pronoun, depending on whether there is a numeral following.

> 我摘了一些苹果。
> *Wǒ zhāi le yì xiē píngguǒ.*
> I picked some apples.

WITHOUT NUMERAL	这些给你，那些给小王。 *Zhè xiē gěi nǐ, nà xiē gěi Xiǎo Wáng.* **These** are for you; **those** are for Xiao Wang.
WITH NUMERAL	这三个给你，那三个给小王。 *Zhè sān ge gěi nǐ, nà sān ge gěi Xiǎo Wáng.* **These three** are for you; **those three** are for Xiao Wang.

English — Interrogative pronouns

Definition   Interrogative pronouns ask a question.

Forms   Interrogative pronouns have different forms for people and things. The pronoun referring to people, *who,* is also inflected for case.

	PEOPLE	THINGS
SUBJECT	*who?*	*which?* *what?*
OBJECT	*whom?*	*which?* *what?*

No change is made for number. *Who?/whom?* and *what?* can refer to one or more than one.

Uses   The interrogative pronouns in English are used in the following ways.

SUBJECT (PERSON)	**Who** *is coming? John.* OR *The Smiths.*
SUBJECT (THING)	**What** *is going on? A riot.*
DIRECT OBJECT (PERSON)	**Whom** *did you see? John.*
DIRECT OBJECT (THING)	**What** *are you doing? My homework.*
INDIRECT OBJECT (PERSON)*	**To whom** *are you speaking? To Mary.*
OBJECT OF A PREPOSITION (PERSON)	**With whom** *are you going? With John.*
OBJECT OF A PREPOSITION (THING)	**What** *are you thinking* **about**? *About the music.*

As an interrogative pronoun, *which?* relates to choice. It can simply be *which?,* used in the singular or plural, or *which one(s)?*

Here are two books. **Which (one)** *do you want?*
There are many good shops in town. **Which (ones)** *do you like best?*

---

*To or for signals the indirect object. (To review the indirect object, see page 14.)

Interrogative pronouns

Forms
Chinese does not distinguish between subject and object in interrogative pronouns; the same forms are used for both.

	PERSON	THING
SINGULAR/PLURAL	谁 *shéi* who/whom	什么 *shénme* what
SINGULAR		哪 *nǎ* (一 *yí*) MW which (one)
PLURAL		哪 *nǎ* 几 *jǐ* MW which (ones)

谁 *shéi* "who/whom" and 什么 *shénme* "what" can refer to one or more than one. The distinction between singular and plural is found only in pronouns that have to do with choosing among two or more possibilities, such as 哪一个 *nǎ yí ge* "which one" and 哪几个 *nǎ jǐ ge* "which ones."

Uses
Unlike in English, an interrogative pronoun in Chinese does not always occur at the beginning of a sentence. Its position in a sentence depends on the function it serves. A subject pronoun occurs in the subject position, and an object pronoun occurs in the object position.

SUBJECT (PERSON)	谁要来？	小王。
	Shéi yào lái?	*Xiǎo Wáng.*
	Who is coming?	Xiao Wang.
SUBJECT (THING)	什么是幸福？	健康。
	Shénme shì xìngfú?	*Jiànkāng.*
	What is happiness?	Being healthy.
DIRECT OBJECT (PERSON)	你看见谁？	阿明。
	Nǐ kànjiàn shéi?	*Āmíng.*
	Whom did you see?	Aming.
DIRECT OBJECT (THING)	你在做什么？	我的功课。
	Nǐ zài zuò shénme?	*Wǒ de gōngkè.*
	What are you doing?	My homework.
INDIRECT OBJECT (PERSON)	这本书你要送给谁？	送给我妹妹。
	Zhè běn shū nǐ yào sòng gěi shéi?	*Sòng gěi wǒ mèimei.*
	To whom do you want to give the book?	To my younger sister.
OBJECT OF A PREPOSITION (PERSON)	你跟谁去？	跟小王。
	Nǐ gēn shéi qù?	*Gēn Xiǎo Wáng.*
	With whom are you going?	With Xiao Wang.
OBJECT OF A PREPOSITION (THING)	一个人的健康跟什么有关？	跟饮食有关。
	Yí gé ren de jiànkāng gēn shénme yǒu guān?	*Gēn yǐnshí yǒu guān.*
	A person's health has to do **with what**?	It has to do with (his) diet.

CONTINUED ON PAGE 40 ▶

哪 *nǎ* (一 *yí*) ᴍᴡ "which (one)" and 哪 *nǎ* 几 *jǐ* ᴍᴡ "which (ones)" are interrogative pronouns of choice. They are used to choose among two or more possibilities.

SINGULAR   这儿有两本书，你要**哪一本**？
*Zhèr yǒu liǎng běn shū. Nǐ yào **nǎ yì běn**?*
Here are two books. Which one do you want?

PLURAL   城内有很多家好的商店，你喜欢**哪几家**？
*Chéngnèi yǒu hěn duō jiā hǎo de shāngdiàn. Nǐ xǐhuan **nǎ jǐ jiā**?*
There are many good shops in town. Which ones do you like?

5

Adjectives

English Introducing adjectives

Definition See page 7.

Forms Some English adjectives are invariable, while others change form. These changes depend on adjective type. The types are discussed separately below.

Uses Adjectives are primarily used as

1. modifiers of nouns or pronouns.

2. complements of either the subject or an object.

An adjective's function determines its position in a sentence.

1. As a modifier, an adjective usually comes before the noun or pronoun that it modifies.

   Buy **that small white house**.
   ADJECTIVES   NOUN

   Buy the **blue**   one.
   ADJECTIVE PRONOUN

2. As a modifier of an indefinite pronoun, an adjective follows the pronoun.

   Something   **terrible** is happening.
   INDEFINITE PRONOUN ADJECTIVE

3. As a subject complement, an adjective follows the verb *to be* or the linking verb and describes the subject.

   Mrs. Li **is**   **happy**.
          FORM OF *to be* ADJECTIVE

   They **seem**   **pleased**.
        LINKING VERB ADJECTIVE

4. As an object complement, an adjective follows the direct object noun or pronoun.

   That made **the exam hard**.
             NOUN   ADJECTIVE

   We considered **him**   **crazy**.
                 PRONOUN ADJECTIVE

Types Each of the following adjective types is discussed separately below.

1. Descriptive (page 44)

2. Proper (a kind of descriptive adjective) (page 48)

3. Limiting (includes demonstratives, possessives, interrogatives, indefinites, numbers, and determiners) (page 48)

Chinese Introducing adjectives

Forms   Chinese adjectives are invariable: they do not change form because of gender, number, or case.

Uses   Adjectives are primarily used as

1. modifiers of nouns or pronouns.

2. complements of an object or a verb.

3. predicates.

An adjective's function determines its position in a sentence.

1. As a modifier, an adjective always comes before the noun or pronoun that it modifies. It is usually followed by the particle 的 *de*.

> 买那座**白的**房子，(或者**蓝的**那座).
> ADJECTIVE + NOUN   ADJECTIVE + PRONOUN + MW
> *Mǎi nà zuò **bái de** fángzi (huòzhě **lán de** nà zuò).*
> Buy that **white** house (or the **blue** one).

2. As an object complement, an adjective follows the direct object noun or pronoun.

> 我喜欢这房子**宽敞**。
> *Wǒ xǐhuan zhè fángzi **kuānchǎng**.*
> I like the house's spaciousness. (LITERALLY, I like the house being **spacious**.)

3. As a verb complement, an adjective follows the particle 得 *de*.

> 他长得很**高**。
> *Tā zhǎng de hěn **gāo**.*
> He is **tall**. (LITERALLY, He grows **tall**.)

4. As a predicate, an adjective occurs in the position where a verb normally occurs.

> 这里夏天很**凉快**。
> *Zhèli xiàtiān hěn **liángkuai**.*
> Here, the summer is **cool**.

NOTE   When an English adjective functions as part of a predicate, it occurs with a verb (for example, "The summer is cool"). In Chinese, no verb is required; the adjective alone is the predicate.

Definition   Descriptive adjectives describe a noun or pronoun.

Forms   Many of these adjectives may be inflected to show comparison (see page 46).

Chinese Descriptive adjectives

Forms In Chinese, descriptive adjectives come in two forms: simple and reduplicated.

	SIMPLE	REDUPLICATED
ONE-SYLLABLE	白 *bái* white	白白 *báibái* whitish
TWO-SYLLABLE	干净 *gānjìng* clean	干干净净 *gāngānjìngjìng* very clean

Uses Reduplication provides a vivid description of the noun or pronoun that it modifies; it has either a moderating or intensifying function. For one-syllable adjectives, reduplication has a moderating effect; for two-syllable adjectives, reduplication has an intensifying effect.

大 *dà* large　　　　大大 *dàdà* largish
硬 *yìng* hard　　　　硬硬 *yìngyìng* kind of hard
高 *gāo* tall　　　　高高 *gāogāo* tallish

简单 *jiǎndān* simple　　简简单单 *jiǎnjiǎndāndān* very simple
快乐 *kuàilè* happy　　快快乐乐 *kuàikuàilèlè* very happy
整齐 *zhěngqí* tidy　　整整齐齐 *zhěngzhěngqíqí* very tidy

Reduplicated forms are always followed by the particle 的 *de,* regardless of their use; simple forms are followed by 的 *de* only when they are used as modifiers.

The four uses of adjectives described on page 43 are illustrated below with reduplicated forms.

1. As a modifier, an adjective always comes before the noun or pronoun that it modifies. It is usually followed by the particle 的 *de.*

    那座**白白的**房子是谁的？
    *Nà zuò **báibái de** fángzi shì shéi de?*
    Who is the owner of that **whitish** house?

2. As an object complement, an adjective follows the direct object noun or pronoun.

    我喜欢这房子**大大的**。
    *Wǒ xǐhuan zhè fángzi **dàdà de**.*
    I like the house's largeness. (LITERALLY, I like the house being **largish**.)

3. As a verb complement, an adjective follows the particle 得 *de.*

    他长得**高高的**。
    *Tā zhǎng de **gāogāo de**.*
    He is **tallish**. (LITERALLY, He grows kind of **tall**.)

4. As a predicate, an adjective occurs in the position where a verb normally occurs.

    这里夏天**凉凉的**。
    *Zhèlǐ xiàtiān **liángliáng de**.*
    Here, the summer is **kind of cool**.

English | Comparison of adjectives

Definition   The three degrees of comparison are positive, comparative, and superlative.

Forms   English forms comparisons in the following ways.

1. Regular comparisons add -*er* and -*est* to short adjectives, sometimes with a minor change in spelling.

   *short ~ short**er** ~ short**est***
   *pretty ~ prett**ier** ~ prett**iest***

2. Longer adjectives are compared by using *more* and *most,* or the negatives *less* and *least*.

   *determined ~ **more** determined ~ **most** determined*
   *obvious ~ **less** obvious ~ **least** obvious*

3. Some adjectives have irregular comparisons.

   good ~ better ~ best
   bad ~ worse ~ worst

4. Adjectives that cannot be compared include absolutes, which are by definition superlative. Uniqueness and perfection cannot be brought to a higher degree.

   unique
   perfect

5. When a comparison is made, several words may introduce the second element: *than, in,* and *of all*.

   COMPARATIVE   *He is taller **than** I (am).*
   SUPERLATIVE   *He is the tallest boy **in** the class. He is the tallest **of all** my students.*

If an adjective is already in the comparative, *more* is not added. Greater contrast may be expressed by words like *much*.

   ***much** smaller*
   ***much** more difficult*

chinese Comparison of adjectives

Forms Adjectives do not change form in comparisons. Regular simple adjectives are used to form the comparative and superlative. Different degrees of comparison are expressed by different structures.

1. For comparatives, three constructions are used.

    MORE THAN [X] 比 *bǐ* [Y] ADJECTIVE
    他比我高。
    Tā bǐ wǒ gāo.
    He is taller than I.

    AS … AS [X] 跟 *gēn* [Y] 一样 *yíyàng* ADJECTIVE
    他跟我一样高。
    Tā gēn wǒ yíyàng gāo.
    He is as tall as I.

    LESS THAN [X] 没有 *méiyǒu* [Y] ADJECTIVE
    他没有我高。
    Tā méiyǒu wǒ gāo.
    He is not as tall as I.

2. Superlatives are formed by adding the adverb 最 *zuì* "most" to simple adjectives.

    高 → 最高
    gāo *zuì gāo*
    tall the tallest

    聪明 → 最聪明
    cōngmíng *zuì cōngmíng*
    intelligent the most intelligent

✓ QUICK CHECK

**Comparative construction with (1) 这些学生 *zhè xiē xuésheng* "these students,"
(2) 那些学生 *nà xiē xuésheng* "those students," and (3) 聪明 *cōngmíng* "intelligent"**

NOUN 1	+ COMPARATIVE	+ NOUN 2	+ ADJECTIVE
这些学生	比	那些学生	聪明
zhè xiē xuésheng	*bǐ*	*nà xiē xuésheng*	*cōngmíng*

These students are more intelligent than those students.

这些学生	跟	那些学生	一样聪明
zhè xiē xuésheng	*gēn*	*nà xiē xuésheng*	*yíyàng cōngmíng*

These students are as intelligent as those students.

这些学生	没有	那些学生	聪明
zhè xiē xuésheng	*méiyǒu*	*nà xiē xuésheng*	*cōngmíng*

These students are less intelligent than those students.

**Superlative construction with (1) 他 *tā* "he," (2) 班上 *bānshàng* "in class,"
and (3) 高 *gāo* "tall"**

NOUN 1	+ VERB	+ PHRASE	+ 最 *zuì*	+ ADJECTIVE	+ 的 *de*	+ NOUN 2
他	是	班上	最	高	的	学生
Tā	*shì*	*bānshàng*	*zuì*	*gāo*	*de*	*xuésheng.*
he	is	in class	most	tall		the student

He is the tallest student in class.

English Proper adjectives

Definition A proper adjective is a descriptive adjective formed from a proper noun (see page 12).

NOUN	ADJECTIVE
China	*Chinese*
Shakespeare	*Shakespearean*

Forms In English, both proper nouns and their adjectives are capitalized. Sometimes, their forms are indistinguishable.

NOUN	ADJECTIVE
the Chinese	*the Chinese people*

English Limiting adjectives

Definition A limiting adjective does not add to your knowledge of a noun; instead, it directs you toward the right one by limiting the choices. The following examples show the types of limiting adjectives.

DEMONSTRATIVE	***this*** *chapter* (not another one)
POSSESSIVE	***his*** *book* (not hers)
INTERROGATIVE	***whose*** *coat?* (its specific owner)
INDEFINITE	***some*** *people* (but not others)
ORDINAL NUMBER	*the **second** lesson* (not the first)

Each of these types of limiting adjectives are discussed separately.

Proper adjectives

Forms Proper adjectives are formed from proper nouns in Chinese. They have the same form as proper nouns.

NOUN	ADJECTIVE
中国	中国文化
Zhōngguó	***Zhōngguó*** *wénhuà*
China	**Chinese** culture
罗马	罗马帝国
Luómǎ	***Luómǎ*** *dìguó*
Rome	**Roman** Empire

 Limiting adjectives

See the discussion on the opposite page.

English Demonstrative adjectives

Definition Demonstrative adjectives point out which of a group is/are the one(s) that you are referring to.

Forms These adjectives have the same forms as the demonstrative pronouns (see page 36) and distinguish in the same way between near and far and between singular and plural.

	SINGULAR	PLURAL
NEAR	*this*	*these*
FAR	*that*	*those*

There is no agreement in person, gender, or case. The demonstrative adjective precedes its noun.

*This woman is talking to **that** man.*
*These little boys hate **those** dogs.*

chinese Demonstrative adjectives

Forms   Demonstrative adjectives have the same forms as demonstrative pronouns (see page 37) and, like the pronouns, distinguish between near and far and between singular and plural.

	SINGULAR	PLURAL	PLURAL WITH NUMERAL
NEAR	这 *zhè* MW	这些 *zhè xiē*	这 *zhè* [numeral] MW
	this	these	these [numeral]
FAR	那 *nà* MW	那些 *nà xiē*	那 *nà* [numeral] MW
	that	those	those [numeral]

Uses   Examples of usage follow.

这位女士在跟**那**位男士说话。
Zhè wèi *nǚshì zài gēn* ***nà wèi*** *nánshì shuō huà.*
This woman is talking to **that** man.

这些小男孩 不喜欢**那些**狗。
Zhè xiē *xiǎo nánhái bù xǐhuan* ***nà xiē*** *gǒu.*
These little boys don't like **those** dogs.

✓ QUICK CHECK

DEMONSTRATIVE ADJECTIVE	NUMERAL	MEASURE WORD	NOUN	ENGLISH MEANING
这 *zhè*	三 *sān*	个 *ge*	苹果 *píngguǒ*	these three apples
那 *nà*	0	杯 *bēi*	水 *shuǐ*	that glass of water
这些 *zhè xiē*	0	0	书 *shū*	these books

English Possessive adjectives

Definition   Possessive adjectives modify a noun by telling to whom or what it belongs.

Forms   These adjectives indicate the person, number, and gender (in the third-person singular) of the *possessor*.

	SINGULAR	PLURAL
FIRST PERSON	*my*	*our*
SECOND PERSON	*your*	*your*
THIRD PERSON	*his, her, its, one's*	*their*

The adjectives do not tell anything about the person or thing that is possessed.

> *Mr. Li's son* → *his* son (third-person singular masculine)
> *Mrs. Li's son* → *her* son (third-person singular feminine)
> *the Lis' son* → *their* son (third-person plural)

Uses   The possessive adjective is always used with the noun.

> *my* mother
> *our* child
> *your* turn

If the noun is omitted, a possessive pronoun must be used (for example, *mine, ours,* or *yours*) (see page 24).

Chinese Adjectival possessive forms

Forms Chinese does not have possessive adjectives. To express possession, the combination of a personal pronoun and the particle 的 *de* is used before the noun. As in English, the pronoun indicates the person, number, and (in the third person) gender of the *possessor*.

	SINGULAR PRONOUN + 的 *de*	PLURAL PRONOUN + 的 *de*
FIRST PERSON	我的 *wǒ de*	我们的 *wǒmen de*
SECOND PERSON	你的 *nǐ de*	你们的 *nǐmen de*
	您的 *nín de*	您的 *nín de*
THIRD PERSON	他的 *tā de* (masc.)	他们的 *tāmen de* (masc.)
	她的 *tā de* (fem.)	她们的 *tāmen de* (fem.)
	它的 *tā de* (inanimate)	它们的 *tāmen de* (inanimate)

Uses The possessive construction (personal pronoun plus the particle 的 *de*) is always used with a noun.

我的爸爸 *wǒ de bàba* my father
我们的孩子 *wǒmen de háizi* our child
你的笔 *nǐ de bǐ* your pen

If the noun is omitted, the pronominal possessive construction (with 的 *de*) is used (see page 25).

我的 *wǒ de* mine
你的 *nǐ de* yours

NOTE If the noun denotes kinship or a close relationship, the particle 的 *de* can be omitted.

我爸爸 *wǒ bàba* my father

English   Interrogative adjectives

Definition   Interrogative adjectives ask a question about limitation.

Forms   These adjectives have case in English.

1. Subject and object cases: *which? what?*

2. Possessive case: *whose?*

These forms are invariable.

Uses   Interrogative adjectives are used

1. to ask a question.

SUBJECT   ***What*** *assignment is for today?*
OBJECT   ***Which*** *class do you have at 10 o'clock?*
POSSESSIVE   ***Whose*** *coat is this?*

2. in an exclamation.

What *a pretty house!*
What *a job!*

chinese Interrogative adjectives

Forms   The form of an interrogative adjective depends on its use in a sentence.

1. Subjective and objective

SINGULAR/PLURAL	什么 *shénme* what	
SINGULAR	哪 *nǎ* (一 *yī*) MW	which (one)
PLURAL	哪些 *nǎ xiē* which (ones)	

2. Possessive

谁 *shéi* (who) + 的 *de* whose

Uses   Interrogative adjectives are used to ask a question, but unlike in English, they are not used in an exclamation. Like interrogative pronouns, interrogative adjectives do not always occur at the beginning of a sentence; their position in a sentence is determined by their function. If they modify the subject, they occur immediately before the subject; if they modify the object, they occur immediately before the object.

今天　有　**什么**　功课?
*Jīntiān yǒu **shénme** gōngkè?*
today　have　**what**　assignment
What is today's assignment?

十　点钟　　你　有　**哪一**　　门　课?
*Shí diǎnzhōng nǐ yǒu **nǎ yì** mén kè?*
10　o'clock　　you have **which one** MW class
Which class do you have at 10 o'clock?

哪些　学生　　要　毕业?
Nǎ xiē xuésheng yào bìyè?
which　students　will　graduate
Which students will graduate?

这　是　**谁的**　上衣?
*Zhè shì **shéi de** shàngyī?*
this　is　**whose**　coat
Whose coat is this?

English Indefinite adjectives

Definition   Indefinite adjectives refer to nouns or pronouns that are not defined more specifically.

> **Some** *students learn fast.*
> **Any** *girl will tell you.*
> **Both** *lectures are at 10 o'clock.*
> **Each/Every** *class has its value.*
> *I want* **another** *pen.*
> **Such** *behavior is terrible.*

Forms   These adjectives are invariable, that is, they do not change their form. Some, however, may be used only with singular nouns (for example, *each, every, another*), some only with plural nouns (for example, *both, other*), and some with either singular or plural nouns (for example, *some*: *some coffee, some people*).

English Other limiting adjectives

Ordinal numbers

These numbers indicate the order in which things come. *One, two,* and *three* (and all numbers ending in *one, two,* and *three,* except *eleven, twelve,* and *thirteen*) have irregular ordinals.

> *first, second, third*

All other ordinal numbers are formed by adding *-th.*

> *fourth, ninth, sixteenth*

Determiners

Determiners are often classified as adjectives (see page 16).

Indefinite adjectives

Forms Some indefinite adjectives directly modify a noun, some combine with a measure word, and still others combine with the particle 的 *de*.

有些学生学得很快。
***Yǒu xiē** xuésheng xué de hěn kuài.*
Some students learn fast.

任何女孩都会告诉你。
***Rènhé** nǚhái dōu huì gàosu nǐ.*
Any girl will tell you.

两个演讲都在十点。
***Liǎng** ge yǎnjiǎng dōu zài shí diǎn.*
Both lectures are at 10 o'clock.

每班有自己的价值观。
***Měi** bān yǒu zìjǐ de jiàzhíguān.*
Each/Every class has its value.

我要另一支笔。
***Wǒ** yào **lìng yì** zhī bǐ.*
I want **another** pen.

这样的行为太不像话了。
***Zhèyàng** de xíngwéi tài bú xiàng huà le.*
Such behavior is terrible.

Other limiting adjectives

Ordinal numbers

Ordinal numbers in Chinese are formed by adding the prefix 第 *dì* to the number (see page 17).

第一 *dì yī* first
第二 *dì èr* second
第三 *dì sān* third
第十 *dì shí* tenth
第十六 *dì shíliù* sixteenth

Determiners

See page 17.

English Other adjectival forms

Many other kinds of words—even though they are not adjectives themselves—may be used as adjectives (that is, to describe a noun or pronoun).

NOUN	a **conference** room
PRESENT PARTICIPLE	**running** water
PAST PARTICIPLE	the **closed** windows
PREPOSITIONAL PHRASE	the poster **on the wall**
RELATIVE CLAUSE	the coat **that I bought**
INFINITIVE	I wonder what **to do**.
ADVERBIAL PHRASE	The students come **from all around**.

chinese Other adjectival forms

Some adjectival forms directly modify a noun, while others combine with the particle 的 *de*.

NOUN
一位**哲学**教授
*yí wèi **zhéxué** jiàoshòu*
a **philosophy** professor

NOUN PHRASE
各地的人都爱戴他。
***Gèdì** de rén dōu àidài tā.*
People everywhere (LITERALLY, **of all places**) love him.

PREPOSITIONAL PHRASE
在墙上的海报
***zài qiángshàng** de hǎibào*
the poster **on the wall**

RELATIVE CLAUSE
我买的海报
***wǒ mǎi** de hǎibào*
the poster **that I bought**

6

Adverbs

English Introducing adverbs

Definition   See page 7.

Forms   Most English adverbs formed from descriptive adjectives add *-ly* to the adjective.

> *active ~ actively*
> *slow ~ slowly*

1. Like adjectives, adverbs may be inflected to show comparison.

POSITIVE	COMPARATIVE	SUPERLATIVE
actively	*more actively*	*most actively*
actively	*less actively*	*least actively*

The comparative is used to show the similarity or difference between how two people or things do something, or the degree of difference in qualifying an adjective or adverb. The superlative compares more than two people or things. There must also be a word to link the two points of comparison.

POSITIVE	*I walk **slowly**.*
COMPARATIVE	*John walks **more slowly than** I do.*
SUPERLATIVE	*Monica walks **the most slowly of** all.*

2. Like adjectives, some adverbs not ending in *-ly* may take *-er* and *-est* in comparisons.

> *He runs fast, but I run **faster**.*
> *Mary runs the **fastest** of all.*

3. Some adverbs form their comparison irregularly.

POSITIVE	COMPARATIVE	SUPERLATIVE
well	*better*	*best*
badly	*worse*	*worst*

Uses   English adverbs are used in the following ways.

1. Adverbs answer the questions *how, when, where,* or *how much* about a verb, an adjective, or another adverb. Sometimes, a phrase takes the place of a single adverb.

> ***Yesterday*** he came **here** and **very**   **quickly** told the story.
> WHEN   WHERE   HOW MUCH   HOW

> ***This morning*** he went **there**   **by car**.
> WHEN   WHERE   HOW

CONTINUED ON PAGE 64 ❯

Introducing adverbs

Forms   Most Chinese adverbs formed from descriptive adjectives add the particle 地 *de* to the adjective.

主动 *zhǔdòng* active → 主动地 *zhǔdòngde* actively
慢慢 *mànmàn* slow → 慢慢地 *mànmànde* slowly

她**主动地**参加各种活动。
Tā zhǔdòngde cānjiā gè zhǒng huódòng.
She **actively** participates in all kinds of activities.

小李**慢慢地**走过来。
Xiǎo Lǐ mànmànde zǒu guòlái.
Xiao Li walked over **slowly**.

Other adverbs include words that indicate the time or place of an event or the manner in which an action is carried out. These adverbs do not have special forms.

明天 *míngtiān* tomorrow
这儿 *zhèr* here

Unlike their English counterparts, Chinese adverbs are not used in comparisons. Adverbial comparisons in English are expressed in Chinese by adjectival complements introduced by the particle 得 *de*.

我走得**很慢**。
Wǒ zǒu de hěn màn.
I walk **slowly**.

小王走得**比我慢**。
Xiǎo Wáng zǒu de bǐ wǒ màn.
Xiao Wang walks **more slowly than I do**.

小李走得**最慢**。
Xiǎo Lǐ zǒu de zuì màn.
Xiao Li walks **the most slowly**.

Uses   Adverbs, regardless of type, always occur before the verb in Chinese.

我　今天　一定　　要　做功课。
Wǒ jītiān yídìng yào zuò gōngkè.
I　today　definitely　will　do homework
I will definitely do homework today.

他 **不停地**　　问问题。
Tā bùtíngde wèn wèntí.
he **continuously** ask questions
He asked questions continuously.

Chinese adverbs are used in the following ways.

1. See the English uses on the opposite page.

昨天他到　　　这儿　　很　　　**快地**讲了一个故事。
WHEN　　　　WHERE　HOW MUCH　HOW
Zuótiān tā dào **zhèr** **hěn** **kuài de** *jiǎng le yí ge gùshi.*
Yesterday he came **here** and **very** **quickly** told the story.

CONTINUED ON PAGE 65 ▶

2. **Negatives**. Some adverbs make a sentence negative. These include words like *not, nowhere,* and *never.* In standard English, two negative words in one sentence express a positive, not a negative, idea.

> *He doesn't have **no** friends, but he has **too few**.*

The first clause used alone and intended as a negative is not standard English. Not only are negative adverbs included here, but negative nouns and adjectives as well.

3. **Questions**. Another group of adverbs introduces questions: *when? where? how?* and *why?* The majority of adverbs answer these questions with respect to the verb, but the interrogative words themselves are adverbs too.

> ***When** does he arrive?*
> ***How** do you know that?*

Many adverbs can also be used as subordinating conjunctions in English (see page 68).

> *We are going to the movies **when** we finish our work.*

Adjectives vs. adverbs

To choose the correct word, it is essential to ask yourself the following questions.

1. Am I *describing someone/something?* → adjective

2. Am I *describing how/when/where/why something is done?* → adverb

> *The **poem** is **good**, and the **poet reads** it **well**.*
> NOUN   ADJECTIVE   VERB   ADVERB

> *The **play** is **bad**, and it's **badly   performed**.*
> NOUN   ADJECTIVE   ADVERB VERB

This is especially important for verbs of mental or emotional state and for sensory verbs, which can be followed by either an adjective or an adverb. One of the most common examples is the following.

> *I feel **bad**.* (= I am sick/unhappy/etc.)
> *I feel **badly**.* (= My hands are not sensitive.)

今天早上他 　　　　跟我到那儿。
WHEN 　　　　　HOW
Jīntiān zǎoshang tā **gēn wǒ** dào nàr.
This morning he **with me** went there.
He went there with me this morning.

✓ QUICK CHECK

An adverbial expression indicating the time or location of an event always precedes the verb.

他	昨天	在小李家	看球赛
SUBJECT	TIME	LOCATION	VERB
Tā	*zuótiān*	*zài Xiǎo Lǐ jiā*	*kàn qiúsài.*
he	yesterday	at Xiao Li's house	watch ball game

He watched a ball game at Xiao Li's house yesterday.

2. **Negatives**

There are three negative forms: 不 *bù*, 没有 *méiyǒu*, and 别 *bié*.

a. 不 *bù* is used in general negation, 没有 *méiyǒu* indicates that an event did not happen, and 别 *bié* is used in imperative sentences.

我不喜欢小王。
*Wǒ **bù** xǐhuan Xiǎo Wáng.*
I do**n't** like XiaoWang.

他没有看见我。
*Tā **méiyǒu** kànjiàn wǒ.*
He did**n't** see me.

别走。
***Bié** zǒu.*
Don't leave.

b. In Chinese, it is more common than in English for a sentence to have more than one negative form.

我不能不去。
*Wǒ **bù** néng **bú** qù.*
I have to go. (LITERALLY, I can**not not** go.)

As in English, the double negation has the effect of producing an affirmative sentence.

3. **Questions**

Question adverbs occur after the subject and before the verb.

他什么时候到?
*Tā **shénme shíhou** dào?*
When does he arrive?

你怎么知道?
*Nǐ **zěnme** zhīdào?*
How do you know that?

CONTINUED ON PAGE 66 ▶

4. **Adverbial clauses**

An adverbial clause of time always occurs before the main clause.

我们工作做完的时候要去看电影。

Wǒmen gōngzuò zuòwán de shíhou yào qù kàn diànyǐng.

When we finish our work, we are going to the movies.

Adjectives vs. adverbs

这首 诗　　很 好,　　　诗人也 读 得 很 好。
　　　NOUN　ADJECTIVE　　　　VERB de　ADJECTIVE

Zhè shǒu shī hěn hǎo, shīrén yě dú de hěn hǎo.

This poem is good, and the poet also reads it well.

这个 剧本 不 好,　　　表演 得 也 不 好。
　　　NOUN　ADJECTIVE VERB de　　　ADJECTIVE

Zhe ge jùběn bù hǎo, biǎoyǎn de yě bù hǎo.

This play is not good, and it is also not well performed.

In both examples above, the nouns and verbs are followed by adjectives, which serve, respectively, as the predicate after the subject and as the predicate complement after the verb + 得 *de* sequence.

Adverbs that describe the manner in which an action is carried out always occur before the verb.

这首 诗　　很 好,　　　诗人 慢慢地 读 着。
　　　NOUN　ADJECTIVE　　　　ADVERB VERB

Zhè shǒu shī hěn hǎo, shīrén mànmande dú zhe.

The poem is good, and the poet reads it slowly.

这个 剧本 不 好,　　　演员 费力地 表演 着。
　　　NOUN　ADJECTIVE　　　ADVERB VERB

Zhè ge jùběn bù hǎo, yǎnyuán fèilìde biǎoyǎn zhe.

This play is not good, and the actors performed with difficulty.

In Chinese, adjectives and adverbs have different forms and do not occur in the same context.

WORD ORDER Adverbs always occur before the verb, while adjective complements describing manner occur after the verb, following the particle 得 *de*. Sometimes, the two orders produce the same meaning.

慢慢地　　走
ADVERB　　VERB

mànmande zǒu

to walk **slowly**

走 得 很慢
VERB de ADJECTIVE COMPLEMENT

zǒu de hěn màn

to walk **slowly** (LITERALLY, in a slow manner)

7

Conjunctions

English — Introducing conjunctions

Definition	See page 7.
Forms	Conjunctions are function words; they are invariable.
Types	All conjunctions are linking words, but the linked elements and their relationship with each other determine which of the three principal types a conjunction belongs to: coordinating, subordinating, or adverbial.
Uses	English conjunctions are used as follows.

1. A **coordinating conjunction** links two equal elements that have the same grammatical construction. The two elements may be single words, phrases, or entire clauses.

NOUNS	*John **and** Mary*
INFINITIVES	*to be **or** not to be*
INDEPENDENT CLAUSES	*We came, **but** he wasn't home.*

   Correlatives, which occur in pairs, are a subgroup of coordinating conjunctions.

   Both *John **and** Mary are in the class.*
   Either *we go now **or** we don't go at all.*

2. A **subordinating conjunction** joins unequal elements. One element is subordinated to the other. The conjunction introduces the subordinate clause (the one that cannot stand alone as a sentence).

CONTRAST	***Although*** *he wants to be on time, he is late.*
TIME	*We speak Chinese **when** our friends come over.*
CAUSE	***Because*** *this course is easy, we all get "A"s.*

   Notice that the main idea of the sentence is in the main (independent) clause. The subordinate clause tells about the time, way, cause, or conditions involved and may show a contrast. Notice also that the main clause need not come first. You could reverse the order of the clauses in each example above without changing the meaning of the sentence.

   There is also a subgroup of correlative subordinating conjunctions (for example, *if . . . then* and *so . . . that*).

   *This course is **so** hard **that** many students have complained.*

3. An **adverbial conjunction** is sometimes called a "conjunctive adverb." Grammarians are not sure whether they are really adverbs or conjunctions. Words and phrases like *therefore, perhaps, also, for example, as a result,* and *in other words* fall into this category.

Chinese Introducing conjunctions

Uses   There are three types of conjunctions in Chinese.

1. Coordinating conjunctions

NOUNS

小王和小李

*Xiǎo Wáng **hé** Xiǎo Lǐ*

Xiao Wang **and** Xiao Li

VERB PHRASES

活着还是死去

*Huó zhe **háishì** sǐqù.*

Be alive **or** die off.

INDEPENDENT CLAUSES

我们来了，但是他不在那儿。

*Wǒmen lái le, **dànshì** tā bú zài nàr.*

We came, **but** he was not there.

Correlative conjunctions are a subgroup of coordinating conjunctions. Chinese has a large number of correlatives; some examples follow.

VERB PHRASES

他不但会说中文，而且会说日文和韩文。

*Tā **búdàn** huì shuō Zhōngwén, **érqiě** huì shuō Rìwén hé Hánwén.*

He **not only** speaks Chinese, **but also** speaks Japanese and Korean.

INDEPENDENT CLAUSES

虽然今天是周末，但是我还得上班。

***Suīrán** jīntiān shì zhōumò, **dànshì** wǒ hái děi shàngbān.*

Although today is the weekend, (**but**) I still need to work.

ADJECTIVES

小李又聪明又漂亮。

*Xiǎo Lǐ **yòu** cōngmíng **yòu** piàoliang.*

Xiao Li is **both** smart **and** pretty.

VERB PHRASES

我弟弟一回到家就打电脑。

*Wǒ dìdi **yī** huí dào jiā **jiù** dǎ diànnǎo.*

As soon as my younger brother gets home, he (**then**) plays on the computer.

2. Subordinating conjunctions

CONTRAST

虽然他走得很快，还是迟到了。

***Suīrán** tā zǒu de hěn kuài, **háishì** chídào le.*

Although he walked fast, he was still late.

TIME

当王家人在的时候，我们说中文。

***Dāng** Wáng jiā rén zài **de shíhou**, wǒmen shuō Zhōngwén.*

When the Wangs are here, we speak Chinese.

CAUSE

因为这门课很容易，我们都得了A。

***Yīnwèi** zhè mén kè hěn róngyì, wǒmen dōu dé le A.*

Because this course is easy, we all get "A"s.

Some conjunctions can be either coordinating or subordinating, depending on whether they occur in pairs or singly in a sentence.

3. Adverbial conjunctions

Following are examples of adverbial conjunctions.

所以 *suǒyǐ* therefore   例如 *lìrú* for example

也许 *yěxǔ* perhaps   也就是说 *yě jiù shì shuō* in other words

Interjections

Introducing interjections

Definition   See page 7.

Forms   Interjections are normally invariable exclamations.

Uses   As an exclamation, an interjection is often merely a sound meant to convey emotion (for example, *ow!*). It has no grammatical connection with the other words in the sentence and is set off by commas.

Chinese Introducing interjections

Following are some common interjections in Chinese.

SURPRISE	啊	*ā*
SIGH	唉	*āi*
SHOCK, SURPRISE	哎呀!	*āiya!*
APPROVAL, AGREEMENT	嗯	*ng*

9

Prepositions

Prepositions in any language are very tricky words. Most of them have basic meanings, but when they are used in phrasal verb constructions, that meaning can change. A phrasal verb is a combination of a verb plus (usually) a preposition that has a meaning different from the combined meanings of the words. You may think, for example, that you know what *up* means, but consider the following sentence.

> *First he cut the tree **down**, then he cut it **up**.*

People learning English would be confused by that sentence, and it is not an isolated example. Take the case of a friend telephoning John's house early in the morning and asking for him. John's wife might reply as follows.

> *He'll be **down** as soon as he's **up**.*

In other words, after learning a preposition and its basic meanings, one must be alert to how it is used in phrasal verb constructions. Often, the meanings of a single preposition will spread over several pages of a dictionary.

Definition See page 7.

Forms A preposition is a function word; it is invariable. It can be a single word or a group of words (for example, *by* and *in spite of*).

Uses A preposition links a noun or pronoun (its object) to other words in the sentence and shows the object's relationship to them. In formal English, a preposition is followed immediately by its object.

> ***to** the store*
> ***about** the subject*

In informal English, a preposition is often placed at the end of the clause or sentence, especially in questions and relative clauses.

> ***What** is she waiting **for**?*
> INSTEAD OF ***For what** is she waiting?*
> *This is the one **that** he is referring **to**.*
> INSTEAD OF *This is the one **to which** he is referring.*

chinese Introducing prepositions

Forms Chinese prepositions have either one or two syllables.

跟 *gēn* with
关于 *guānyú* about

Uses Prepositions typically occur with noun phrases to form prepositional phrases. Such phrases usually occur in three positions in a sentence.

1. Most prepositional phrases occur *after* the subject and *before* the verb. In this position, a prepositional phrase modifies the action of the verb, indicating the location, time, or another aspect of the action.

   小王**在**图书馆看书。
   *Xiǎo Wáng **zài** túshūguǎn kàn shū.*
   Xiao Wang is reading **in** the library.

   我**从**中国来。
   *Wǒ **cóng** Zhōngguó lái.*
   I come **from** China.

2. A few prepositional phrases can also occur *after* the verb and serve as complements.

   到 *dào* to (destination)
   向 *xiàng* toward (direction)
   在 *zài* at/in/on (location)
   给 *gěi* to (recipient)

   In the following sentences, the prepositional phrases indicate the location of the object as a result of the action.

   我送小李**到**机场。
   *Wǒ sòng Xiǎo Lǐ **dào** jīchǎng.*
   I took Xiao Li **to** the airport.

   他把书放**在**桌上。
   *Tā bǎ shū fàng **zài** zhuō shang.*
   He put the book **on** the table.

3. Certain prepositional phrases may occur *at the beginning of* a sentence. In this position, they establish the topic of the sentence, indicating what the sentence is about.

   关于开会的事，我还没有收到通知。
   ***Guānyú** kāihuì de shì, wǒ hái méiyǒu shōu dào tōngzhī.*
   About the meeting, I have not received a notice.

   对于这本书，我没有意见。
   ***Duìyú** zhè běn shū, wǒ méiyǒu yìjiàn.*
   About this book, I have no opinion.

CONTINUED ON PAGE 78 ▶

Some special problems with prepositions

Historically, most Chinese prepositions are derived from verbs, and in modern Chinese, many prepositions can still function as verbs. To decide if a form is used as a preposition or a verb, the structure of the sentence must be considered.

圣诞节　　　到　　了。

　　　　　　VERB

*Shèngdànjié **dào** le.*

Christmas has **arrived**.

我　到　　　　学校　去　借　　书。

　　PREPOSITION　　　VERB　VERB

*Wǒ **dào** xuéxiào **qù** **jiè** shū.*

I **to** school **go** **borrow** books

I **went to** the school to **borrow** books.

他　给　　了我一本书。

　　VERB

*Tā **gěi** le wǒ yì běn shū.*

He **gave** me a book.

他　寄　了一本书　给　　　　我。

　　VERB　　　　　　PREPOSITION

*Tā **jì** le yì běn shū **gěi** wǒ.*

He **sent** a book **to** me.

10

Verbs

English Introducing verbs

Definition   See page 7.

Forms   English has very few inflected verb forms. Many English verbs have only four forms (for example, *talk, talks, talked, talking*); some have five forms (for example, *sing, sings, sang, sung, singing*).

In some systems of grammar, it is said that, technically, English has only two tenses—present and past—and that other temporal concepts are expressed by periphrastic verbal constructions. This means that English uses helping verbs and other expressions to convey temporal differences. Verbs are presented here in a more traditional way, because it will help you see the parallels between English and Chinese constructions. Following are the principal parts of an English verb.

INFINITIVE	SIMPLE PAST	PAST PARTICIPLE	PRESENT PARTICIPLE
talk	*talked*	*talked*	*talking*
sing	*sang*	*sung*	*singing*

Some words used to identify verb forms are **conjugation**, **tense**, **voice**, **transitive**, **intransitive**, and **mood**.

Conjugation

This word has two meanings.

1. In Latin and in modern Romance languages, verbs are classified into groups, or conjugations, by their infinitive endings. English and German have only *regular* and *irregular* (sometimes called *weak* and *strong*) verbs. Weak verbs take a regular ending to form the past (for example, *talk ~ talked* and *follow ~ followed*). Strong verbs often change the vowel in their past forms, and some past forms may look completely different from their infinitives (for example, *sing ~ sang* and *go ~ went*).

2. Conjugation also refers to a list, by person, of each form in a given tense. In English, verbs can be conjugated but usually are not, because there is only one inflected ending: *-s* is added to the third-person singular of the simple present tense.

	SINGULAR	PLURAL
FIRST PERSON	*I speak*	*we speak*
SECOND PERSON	*you speak*	*you speak*
THIRD PERSON	*he/she speaks*	*they speak*

A noun or pronoun is required with every verb form, because otherwise it would not be known who or what the subject is.

Tense

This word comes from Latin *tempus* via French *temps,* meaning "time." The tense tells *when* something happened, *how long* it lasted, and whether it is *completed*.

CONTINUED ON PAGE 82 ▶

Chinese Introducing verbs

Forms   Verbs are not inflected in Chinese. They have the same form, regardless of the person or number of the subject, the time that an event occurred, or the part of an event that is being described. To convey differences comparable to tense differences in English, Chinese uses a variety of expressions, including aspect markers, modal verbs, and time adverbials.

我　昨天　去　了　　　　　学校。
　　ADVERB　VERB　ASPECT MARKER

*Wǒ **zuótiān** **qù** **le**　　　xuéxiào.*

I **went** to school **yesterday**.

我　明天　要　　　去　学校。
　　ADVERB　MODAL VERB　VERB

*Wǒ **míngtiān** **yào**　　　**qù**　xuéxiào.*

I **will go** to school **tomorrow**.

Conjugation

Chinese verbs are not conjugated.

Tense

Chinese verbs do not indicate tense. As shown in the examples above, the same verb form is used to describe both past and future events.

Aspect

Chinese uses aspect to indicate whether an event is completed, in progress, or at some other stage. There are four major aspect markers.

IMPERFECTIVE	在 *zài*	The event is ongoing and dynamic.	
	着 *zhe*	The event is ongoing and static.	
PERFECTIVE	了 *le*	The event is viewed as a whole, including its beginning and end.	
	过 *guò*	The event was completed some time ago.	

CONTINUED ON PAGE 83 ▶

Voice

English has two voices: active and passive. **Active voice** means that the subject is or is doing something.

>*Mary is happy.*
>*Mary reads the newspaper.*

In these examples, *Mary* is the subject.

Passive voice means that the subject is acted on by an agent. The verb tells what happens to the subject.

>*The newspaper is read by Mary.*

In this example, *newspaper* is the subject.

Transitive verbs

These verbs require an object to express a complete meaning.

>*Mr. White surprised a burglar.*

In this example, the verb *surprised* is transitive, because it takes an object, *burglar*. If we omitted the object, the sentence would not make sense; it would be incomplete.

Intransitive verbs

These verbs do not require an object.

>*Paul sat down.*

Here, the verb *sat* is intransitive, because it has no object; *down* is an adverb.

English has many verbs that can be either transitive or intransitive.

Peter	**eats**	*dinner*	*at 7 o'clock.*
The butcher	**weighs**	*the meat.*	
SUBJECT	TRANSITIVE VERB	DIRECT OBJECT	

Peter	**eats**	*at 7 o'clock.*
The butcher	**weighs**	*a lot.*
SUBJECT	INTRANSITIVE VERB	

Mood

This grammatical concept indicates the mood, or attitude, of the speaker. Is the speaker stating a fact? Giving an order? Offering a possibility that has not happened yet? Making a recommendation? Three moods are used to express these ideas: indicative, imperative, and subjunctive. The indicative is by far the most common mood.

Voice

The passive voice is not used in Chinese as frequently as it is in English, although a sentence where the object is affected is more likely to use the passive form.

玛丽看报纸。
Mǎlì kàn bàozhǐ.
Mary reads the newspaper.

The sentence above does not have a corresponding passive form. It can only be formed with 玛丽 *Mǎlì* as the subject and 报纸 *bàozhǐ* as the object. The following sentence, however, can be changed into the passive voice.

小王弄坏了我的电脑。(小王 *Xiǎo Wáng* is the subject.)
Xiǎo Wáng nòng huài le wǒ de diànnǎo.
Xiao Wang broke my computer.

我的电脑**被**小王弄坏了。(我的电脑 *Wǒ de diànnǎo* is the subject.)
*Wǒ de diànnǎo **bèi** Xiǎo Wáng nòng huài le.*
My computer was broken by Xiao Wang.

Transitive and intransitive verbs

Whether a verb that describes a particular action is transitive or intransitive varies between languages. Certain intransitive verbs in English correspond to transitive verbs in Chinese.

ENGLISH INTRANSITIVE VERB	CHINESE TRANSITIVE VERB	OBJECT
walk	走 walk *zǒu*	路 road *lù*
sleep	睡 sleep *shuì*	觉 sleep *jiào*
dance	跳 jump *tiào*	舞 dance *wǔ*
sing	唱 sing *chàng*	歌 song *gē*

Mood

Chinese has two moods: indicative and imperative. The verb form is the same, regardless of the mood.

Forms There are four ways to ask a question in English.

1. Place a question mark after a statement and raise the pitch of your voice at the end of the statement when saying it aloud.

   Anne is here already?
   That's Mark's idea?

2. Add a "tag," repeating the verb or auxiliary verb as a negative question. In English, the specific tag depends on the subject and the verb.

   *Peter is happy, **isn't he**?*
   *Anna finished studying, **didn't she**?*

3. Invert the subject and an auxiliary or modal verb or the verb *to be*.

PRESENT	***Do you** have any brothers?*
PRESENT PROGRESSIVE	***Is Peter** buying his books?*
PRESENT	***Does Peter** buy his books?*
PRESENT PERFECT	***Has Peter** bought his books?*
PRESENT	***May I** see you this evening?*
PRESENT	***Is Robert** here today?*

4. Use an interrogative word.

   ***Where** is the library?*
   ***When** does the library open?*

Chinese Introducing questions

Forms There are six ways to ask a question in Chinese.

1. Place the question marker 吗 *ma* after a statement.

   安妮已经在这儿了**吗**？
   *Ānní yǐjīng zài zhèr le **ma**?*
   Is Anne already here?

   这是马克的主意**吗**？
   *Zhè shì Mǎkè de zhǔyì **ma**?*
   Is this Mark's idea?

2. Place a negation word and a repeated verb or verb phrase immediately after the verb or verb phrase to form a question that expects a "yes" or "no" answer.

   你 有 没 有 兄弟？
   　　VERB NEGATION VERB
   *Nǐ **yǒu méi yǒu** xiōngdì?*
   Do you have (any) brothers?

   彼得买 不 买 书？
   　　VERB NEGATION VERB
   *Bǐdé **mǎi bù mǎi** shū?*
   Does Peter buy books or not?

CONTINUED ON PAGE 85 ▶

彼得	买书	不	买书？
	VERB PHRASE	NEGATION	VERB PHRASE

Bǐdé **mǎi shū** *bù* **mǎi shū?**

Does Peter buy books or not?

3. Place a tag question after a statement. In Chinese, each tag has an invariable form, regardless of the subject or verb. There are several tags, including the following.

彼得很开心，**是吗**？

Bǐdé hěn kāixīn, **shì ma?**

Peter is happy, isn't he?

彼得很开心，**是不是**？

Bǐdé hěn kāixīn, **shì bú shì?**

Peter is happy, isn't he?

他们准时到达了，**对吗**？

Tāmen zhǔnshí dàodá le, **duì ma?**

They arrived on time, right?

他们准时到达了，**对不对**？

Tāmen zhǔnshí dàodá le, **duì bú duì?**

They arrived on time, right?

你在这儿等我，**好吗**？

Nǐ zài zhèr děng wǒ, **hǎo ma?**

You wait for me here, okay?

你在这儿等我，**好不好**？

Nǐ zài zhèr děng wǒ, **hǎo bù hǎo?**

You wait for me here, okay?

4. Place the conjunction 还是 *háishì* "or" between two or more words or phrases.

NOUNS 你喜欢喝茶、可乐**还是**咖啡？

Nǐ xǐhuān hē chá, kělè **háishì** *kāfēi?*

Do you like to drink tea, Coke, or coffee?

VERB PHRASES 彼得 买书**还是**不买书？

Bǐdé mǎi shū **háishì** *bù mǎi shū?*

Does Peter buy books or not buy books?

5. Use an interrogative word.

图书馆在**哪儿**？

Túshūguǎn zài **nǎr?**

Where is the library?

图书馆**什么时候**开门？

Túshūguǎn **shénme shíhou** *kāi mén?*

When is the library open?

6. Use the particle 呢 *ne* after a noun phrase to ask a reduced-form question as a follow-up to a previous statement.

我很好，你**呢**？

Wǒ hěn hǎo, nǐ **ne?**

I'm fine. How about you?

小李和小王都到了，小张**呢**？

Xiǎo Lǐ hé Xiǎo Wáng dōu dào le, Xiǎo Zhāng **ne?**

Xiao Li and Xiao Wang are both here. What about Xiao Zhang?

Word order

Except for tag questions and questions with 呢 *ne* that have a reduced form, the word order for questions is exactly the same as for a statement. The question marker 吗 *ma* is added to the end of a statement, and an interrogative word simply takes the position of a non-interrogative word.

Introducing verbals

Definition   Verbals are forms of the verb that are not finite, that is, do not agree with a subject and do not function as the predicate of a sentence. There are five types of verbals: present infinitive, past infinitive, gerund, present participle, and past participle.

English Present infinitives

Definition   The present infinitive is the basic form of the verb, as it appears in a dictionary.

Forms   The infinitive is often identified by the word *to* preceding it. However, *to* is omitted in many infinitive constructions, especially after verbs like *can* and *let*. Compare the following sentences, both of which contain the infinitive *swim*.

> *I know how* **to swim**.
> *I can* **swim**.

Uses   In addition to completing the verb, as in the above examples, an infinitive may serve as the subject or object of a sentence, as an adjective, or as an adverb.

SUBJECT	**To err** *is human.*
OBJECT	*He hopes* **to come** *soon.*
ADJECTIVE	*English is the subject* **to study**.
ADVERB	**To tell** *the truth, I don't believe her.*

Infinitives may also have their own direct objects and other modifiers.

> *I am able* **to do** *that   easily.*
>   DIRECT OBJECT ADVERB

English Past infinitives

Forms   The past infinitive is formed with the present infinitive of the auxiliary verb plus the past participle of the main verb.

> *to go* (present infinitive) → *to have gone* (past infinitive)

Uses   The past infinitive is used in the same ways as the present infinitive.

> **To have quit** *is terrible.*

CONTINUED ON PAGE 88 ▶

Chinese Verbal equivalents

Forms Chinese does not have verbals. Since verbs are invariable, they do not have nonfinite forms, such as infinitives, gerunds, or participles. In Chinese, the functions of English verbals are performed by verbs, sometimes in combination with objects, modifiers, and auxiliary verbs.

Uses Besides its function as the predicate of a sentence, the Chinese verb has several other uses.

1. Subject

   走路对你好。
   ***Zǒu lù** duì nǐ hǎo.*
   Walking is good for you.

2. Object

   他希望很快就**来**。
   *Tā xīwàng hěn kuài jiù **lái**.*
   He hopes **to come** soon.

   我喜欢**运动**。
   *Wǒ xǐhuan **yùndòng**.*
   I like **to exercise**.

3. Adjective

   英文是该**研读**的科目。
   *Yīngwén shì gāi **yándú** de kēmù.*
   English is the subject **to study**.

   一个会**说话**的洋娃娃
   *yí ge huì **shuō huà** de yáng wáwa*
   a **talking** doll

   一个已被**证明**的事实
   *yí ge yǐ bèi **zhèngmíng** de shìshí*
   a **proven** fact

4. Adverb

   说实话，他非常想要那个东西。
   ***Shuō shí huà**, tā fēicháng xiǎng yào nà ge dōngxi.*
   To tell the truth, he wants that thing very much.

CONTINUED ON PAGE 89 ▶

English Gerunds

Definition Gerunds are often called verbal nouns.

Forms The English gerund is formed by adding *-ing* to the infinitive form of the verb.

> *sing* → *singing*
> *run* → *running*
> *bite* → *biting*

Uses Gerunds have the same functions as other nouns (see page 10).

> SUBJECT **Walking** is good for you.
> OBJECT I like **singing**.

Gerunds may also have objects and modifiers.

> **Making** money   quickly is many people's goal.
>   DIRECT OBJECT ADVERB

English Participles

Definition Participles are verbal adjectives that constitute the third and fourth principal parts of a verb.

Forms English has two participles.

1. **Present participles** (the fourth principal part) end in *-ing*.

   > *singing*
   > *talking*
   > *managing*

2. **Past participles** (the third principal part) end in *-ed* or *-n* for regular verbs.

   > *tried*
   > *gathered*
   > *concentrated*
   > *given*

   To determine the past participle of an irregular verb, say, "Today I go; yesterday I went; I have gone; I am going." The form used after "I have" is the past participle. In the dictionary, the principal parts are given for every irregular verb.

Uses The two types of participles have the same basic uses.

1. As part of a compound verb (one consisting of two or more words)

   > PRESENT PROGRESSIVE He **is talking**.
   > PAST PERFECT They **have given**.

2. As an adjective

   > a **talking** doll
   > a **proven** fact

3. In an absolute phrase modifying a noun

   > **Walking** along the street, he met Robin.
   > **Seen** from the front, the building was even more imposing.

   In the two examples above, *he* is *walking* and *the building* was *seen*.

5. In an adjectival clause

> **走**在街上，他遇见了罗彬。
> ***Zǒu** zài jīeshang, tā yùjiàn le Luóbīn.*
> **Walking** on the street, he met Robin.

> 从前面**看**，这栋大楼显得更有气势。
> *Cóng qiánmiàn **kàn**, zhè dòng dàlóu xiǎn de gèng yǒu qìshì.*
> **Seen** from the front, the building was even more imposing.

In the two examples above, *he* is *walking* and *the building* was *seen*.

Indicative mood

The verbs on pages 90–123 are all in the indicative mood. It is the mood used for stating facts and for making assertions as though they were facts.

English Present tense

Definition   The present tense is defined by its uses (see page 92).

Forms   There are three present tenses in English: simple present, present progressive, and present emphatic.

1. **Simple present.** There is only one inflected form in the simple present: the third-person singular, which adds *-s* to the basic verb form.

	SINGULAR	PLURAL
FIRST PERSON	*I sing*	*we sing*
SECOND PERSON	*you sing*	*you sing*
THIRD PERSON	*he/she sings*	*they sing*

2. **Present progressive.** This tense is formed with the present tense of *to be* plus the present participle.

	SINGULAR	PLURAL
FIRST PERSON	*I am singing*	*we are singing*
SECOND PERSON	*you are singing*	*you are singing*
THIRD PERSON	*he/she is singing*	*they are singing*

3. **Present emphatic.** This tense is formed with the present tense of *to do* plus the infinitive.

	SINGULAR	PLURAL
FIRST PERSON	*I do sing*	*we do sing*
SECOND PERSON	*you do sing*	*you do sing*
THIRD PERSON	*he/she does sing*	*they do sing*

CONTINUED ON PAGE 92 ▶

Chinese Present-time actions and states

Forms   The following chart shows the aspect markers for verbs of present-time actions and states.

PRESENT ACTION/STATE	PRESENT PROGRESSIVE	PRESENT DURATIVE	PRESENT EMPHATIC
Verb	在 *zài* + Verb 正在 *zhèngzài* + Verb	Verb + 着 *zhe*	是 *shì* + Verb

1. **Present action or state.** The verb has no accompanying auxiliary verb or aspect marker.

   她唱歌。
   Tā chàng gē.
   She sings.

   他们唱歌。
   Tāmen chàng gē.
   They sing.

2. **Progressive aspect.** The progressive marker 在 *zài* or 正在 *zhèngzài* is placed immediately before the verb.

   她在唱歌。
   Tā zài chàng gē.
   She is singing.

   他们正在唱歌。
   Tāmen zhèngzài chàng gē.
   They are singing.

3. **Durative aspect.** The durative marker 着 *zhe* is placed immediately after the verb.

   她戴着手套。
   Tā dàizhe shǒutào.
   She is wearing gloves.

   他们戴着手套。
   Tāmen dàizhe shǒutào.
   They are wearing gloves.

4. **Emphatic.** The verb 是 *shì* "to be" is placed immediately before the verb.

   我是喜欢他。
   Wǒ shì xǐhuan tā.
   I do like him.

   我们是喜欢他。
   Wǒmen shì xǐhuan tā.
   We do like him.

CONTINUED ON PAGE 93 ▶

Uses   The **simple present** is used for

1. an action or state occurring in the present.

   *They **speak** Chinese.*

2. a habitual action that is still true.

   *I always **study** in the evening.*

3. existing facts and eternal truths.

   *Beijing **is** the capital of China.*
   *I **think**, therefore I **am**.* (René Descartes)

The **present progressive** is used to

1. stress the continuing nature of the verb's action in either a statement or a question.

   *I **am** still **trying**!*
   *Are you **going** to the library now?*

2. make a future action seem more immediate.

   *We **are reading** this book next week.*
   *I **am going** to the show tomorrow.*

The **present emphatic** is used to

1. add emphasis or contradict.

   *I **do want** to do well.*
   *They **do** not **do** that!*

2. form questions or negative statements.

   ***Do** you **go** to the lake in the summer?*
   *I **do** not **know** what you are talking about.*

Uses 1. Verbs with no accompanying auxiliary verbs or aspect markers have functions similar to the simple present tense in English, including

    a. an action occurring in the present.

      他们**说**中文。
      *Tāmen **shuō** Zhōngwén.*
      They **speak** Chinese.

    b. a habitual action.

      我总是在晚上**念**书。
      *Wǒ zǒngshì zài wǎnshang **niàn** shū.*
      I always **study** in the evening.

    c. existing facts and external truths.

      北京**是**中国的首都。
      *Běijīng **shì** Zhōngguó de shǒudū.*
      Beijing **is** the capital of China.

2. The progressive aspect is used to stress the continuing nature of the verb's action.

    我仍然**在努力**。
    *Wǒ réngrán **zài nǔlì**.*
    I'm still **trying**.

    NOTE Unlike in English, the progressive aspect cannot be used to describe an immediate future action in Chinese. This is described by the auxiliary verb 要 *yào* "will."

    我们下星期**要读**这本书。
    *Wǒmen xià xīngqī **yào dú** zhè běn shū.*
    We **are going to read** the book next week.

    我明天**要去看**表演。
    *Wǒ míngtiān **yào qù kàn** biǎoyǎn.*
    I'm going to watch the show tomorrow.

3. The durative aspect is used to stress the continuing nature of the state described by the verb.

    墙上**挂着**一幅画。
    *Qiángshàng **guà zhe** yì fú huà.*
    There is a painting hanging on the wall.

4. The emphatic is used to add emphasis to a statement.

    我**是**想做好。
    *Wǒ **shì** xiǎng zuò hǎo.*
    I **do** want to do well.

    他们**是**不在这儿！
    *Tāmen **shì** bú zài zhèr!*
    They **are** not here!

NOTE Unlike in English, the emphatic cannot be used to form questions or negative statements in Chinese.

    ✓ *QUICK CHECK*

在 *zài* and 正在 *zhèngzài* occur before the verb.
着 *zhe* occurs after the verb.

English Past tense

Definition The past tense describes actions or states in the past.

Forms There are three past tenses, each corresponding to one of the three present tenses discussed in the previous section. (For perfect tenses, see pages 104–120.)

1. The **simple past** is the second principal part of the verb (see page 80). It is not inflected; all of the forms are the same. The simple past of weak verbs ends in *-ed* (for example, *talked* and *wished*). Strong verbs have irregular past forms.

	SINGULAR	PLURAL
FIRST PERSON	*I sang*	*we sang*
SECOND PERSON	*you sang*	*you sang*
THIRD PERSON	*he/she sang*	*they sang*

2. The **past progressive** is formed with the simple past of the verb *to be* plus the present participle of the main verb.

	SINGULAR	PLURAL
FIRST PERSON	*I was singing*	*we were singing*
SECOND PERSON	*you were singing*	*you were singing*
THIRD PERSON	*he/she was singing*	*they were singing*

3. The **past emphatic** is formed with the simple past of the verb *to do* plus the infinitive.

	SINGULAR	PLURAL
FIRST PERSON	*I did sing*	*we did sing*
SECOND PERSON	*you did sing*	*you did sing*
THIRD PERSON	*he/she did sing*	*they did sing*

CONTINUED ON PAGE 96 ▶

Forms   The following chart shows the aspect markers for verbs of past actions and states.

PAST ACTION	PAST STATE OR HABITUAL PAST ACTION	PAST PROGRESSIVE	PAST DURATIVE	PAST EMPHATIC
Adv…Verb + 了 *le*	Adv…Verb	Adv…在 *zài* + Verb Adv…正在 *zhèngzài* + Verb	Adv…Verb + 着 *zhe*	是 *shì* + Verb

1. **Past action.** The verb is often marked with the perfective marker 了 *le*.

   昨天我们**看了**一个电影。

   *Zuótiān wǒmen **kàn le** yí ge diànyǐng.*

   We **watched** a movie yesterday.

   NOTE   The perfective marker 了 *le* is not always used for a past action. Its use depends on a number of factors, including the type of verb, the sentence structure, and context. Following is a sentence in which 了 *le* is not used.

   他昨天**告诉**我们他在图书馆工作。

   *Zuótiān tā **gàosù** wǒmen tā zài túshūguǎn gōngzuò.*

   He **told** us yesterday that he works in the library.

2. **Past state or habitual past action.** The verb is not marked. The past meaning is conveyed by an adverb of time.

PAST STATE	昨天**是**星期天。
	*Zuótiān **shì** xīngqī tiān.*
	It **was** Sunday yesterday. / Yesterday **was** Sunday.
PAST STATE	她昨天**感到**很高兴。
	*Tā zuótiān **gǎndào** hěn gāoxìng.*
	She **felt** happy yesterday.
HABITUAL PAST ACTION	我**以前**每天都**见到**他。
	*Wǒ **yǐqián** měi tiān dōu **jiàndào** tā.*
	I **used to see** him every day.

3. **Past progressive aspect.** The progressive marker 在 *zài* or 正在 *zhèngzài* is placed immediately before the verb, in the same way that a present-time event is marked. The past meaning is conveyed by an adverb of time.

   我刚才**在唱歌**。

   *Wǒ gāngcái **zài chàng gē**.*

   I **was singing** just now.

   If there is no adverb of time, a progressive sentence could describe either a present-time or a past event.

   我**正在唱歌**。

   *Wǒ **zhèngzài chàng gē**.*

   I **am singing**. OR I **was singing**.

CONTINUED ON PAGE 97 ▶

Uses The three past tenses closely parallel the three present tenses in usage, except that the action takes place in the past. The simple past states a fact, the past progressive emphasizes the duration or continuation of an action at a given moment in the past, and the past emphatic stresses a statement and is used to form negatives and questions.

Other past forms

Other expressions provide special past meanings.

1. Immediate past action: *to have just* plus the past participle

   *Mary **has just arrived** this minute.*

2. Habitual past action: *used to* or *would* plus the infinitive

   *I **used to go** to the movies every week.*
   *For a long time, I **would see** them every day.*

3. Repeated past action: *kept (on)* plus the present participle

   *He **kept (on) doing** it.*

4. **Past durative aspect**. The durative marker 着 *zhe* is placed immediately after the verb, in the same way that a present-time state is marked. The past meaning is conveyed by an adverb of time.

> 她刚才**戴着**手套。
> *Tā gāngcái **dài zhe** shǒutào.*
> She **was wearing** gloves just now.

5. **Past emphatic**. The verb 是 *shì* "to be" is placed immediately before the verb.

> 我以前**是喜欢**他。
> *Wǒ yǐqián **shì xǐhuan** tā.*
> I **did like** him before.

> 我们以前**是喜欢**他。
> *Wǒmen yǐqián **shì xǐhuan** tā.*
> We **did like** him before.

Uses

1. A verb that is marked by 了 *le* and occurs with an adverb of past time describes a past action.

2. A verb that is not marked and occurs with an adverb of past time describes a past state or a habitual past action.

3. A verb that is marked by 在 *zài* or 正在 *zhèngzài* and occurs with an adverb of past time describes the continuation of an action in the past.

4. A verb that is marked by 着 *zhe* and occurs with an adverb of past time describes the duration of a state in the past.

5. The past emphatic is used to add emphasis to a past statement.

Other past forms

1. Immediate past action: 刚 *gāng* "just now" + verb

> 玛丽**刚到**。
> *Mǎlì **gāng dào**.*
> Mary **has just arrived**.

2. Repeated past action: 一直 *yìzhí* "continuously" + the progressive form 在 *zài* + verb

> 他**一直在做**这个。
> *Tā **yìzhí zài zuò** zhè ge.*
> He **kept doing** this.

3. Continued past state: 一直 *yìzhí* "continuously" + verb + the durative form 着 *zhe*

> 昨天门**一直开着**。
> *Zuótiān mén **yìzhí kāi zhe**.*
> The door **was kept open** yesterday.

English Future tense

Definition The future tense describes events that have not yet taken place.

Forms There are only two tenses for future time: the future and the future progressive. Both are compound tenses, that is, they require more than one word to form them.

1. The **future tense** is formed by using the auxiliary verb *will* plus the infinitive of the main verb.

	SINGULAR	PLURAL
FIRST PERSON	*I will sing*	*we will sing*
SECOND PERSON	*you will sing*	*you will sing*
THIRD PERSON	*he/she will sing*	*they will sing*

2. The **future progressive tense** is formed with the future of *to be* plus the present participle. It therefore requires three words.

	SINGULAR	PLURAL
FIRST PERSON	*I will be singing*	*we will be singing*
SECOND PERSON	*you will be singing*	*you will be singing*
THIRD PERSON	*he/she will be singing*	*they will be singing*

NOTES

1. There are no irregular future tense forms in English.

2. *Will* is often contracted to *'ll*.

> *We'**ll** do it tomorrow.*
> *You'**ll** be studying that next week.*

CONTINUED ON PAGE 100 ▶

Chinese Future actions and states

Forms The following chart shows the aspect markers for verbs of future actions and states.

INTENTIONAL	NONINTENTIONAL	FUTURE PROGRESSIVE	FUTURE DURATIVE
要 *yào* + Verb	会 *huì* + Verb	会在 *huì zài* + Verb 可能在 *kěnéng zài* + Verb 可能会在 *kěnéng huì zài* + Verb	会 *huì* + Verb + 着 *zhe* 可能 *kěnéng* + Verb + 着 *zhe* 可能会 *kěnéng huì* + Verb + 着 *zhe*

NOTES 在 *zài* can be replaced by 正在 *zhèngzài*. 可能 *kěnéng* "possibly" can be replaced by other adverbs that indicate different degrees of possibility, for example, 也许 *yěxǔ* "maybe" and 一定 *yídìng* "certainly."

1. **Intentional event.** The auxiliary verb 要 *yào* "will" is placed before the verb if the focus is on the intention of the subject.

   我们**要唱歌**。
   *Wǒmen **yào chàng gē**.*
   We **will sing**.

2. **Nonintentional event.** The auxiliary verb 会 *huì* "will" is placed before the verb if the focus is on the possibility of a future action or state.

   明天**会下雨**。
   *Míngtiān **huì xià yǔ**.*
   It **will rain** tomorrow.

   我弟弟下星期**会来看**我。
   *Wǒ dìdi xià xīngqī **huì lái kàn** wǒ.*
   My younger brother **will come to visit** me next week.

   你**会有**很多朋友。
   *Nǐ **huì yǒu** hěn duō péngyǒu.*
   You **will have** many friends.

3. **Future progressive aspect.** An adverb expressing possibility (for example, 可能 *kěnéng* "possibly," the auxiliary 会 *huì* "will," or both) is placed immediately before the progressive form 在 *zài* + verb.

   十年后你**会在做**什么?
   *Shí nián hòu, nǐ **huì zài zuò** shénme?*
   What **will** you **be doing** 10 years from now?

   他来的时候，我**可能(会)在打**球。
   *Tā lái de shíhou, wǒ **kěnéng (huì) zài dǎ** qiú.*
   When he comes, I **might be playing** ball.

4. **Future durative aspect.** An adverb expressing possibility (for example, 可能 *kěnéng* "possibly," the auxiliary 会 *huì* "will," or both) is placed immediately before the verb + durative marker 着 *zhe*.

   明天的聚会，我**会戴着**你给我的项链。
   *Míngtiān de jùhuì, wǒ **huì dài zhe** nǐ gěi wǒ de xiàngliàng.*
   At tomorrow's gathering, I **will be wearing** the necklace you gave me.

   晚上这个门**可能会开着**。
   *Wǎnshàng zhè ge mén **kěnéng huì kāi zhe**.*
   This door **may be open** in the evening.

CONTINUED ON PAGE 101 ▶

Uses   The distinction between the future and future progressive tenses is the same as that between the corresponding present tenses (see page 92). They are used

1. to express an action or state that will happen or exist in the future.

2. in Type 1 conditional sentences, where the *if* clause is in the present. (See the **Quick Check** on page 120.)

   *If you **study**, you **will succeed**.*

Other future forms

Another way to express future action is an idiomatic use of *to go* plus the infinitive of the main verb.

   *I **am going to sing** tomorrow.*

Uses

1. A verb that occurs with 要 *yào* "will" focuses on the intention of the subject.

2. A verb that occurs with 会 *huì* "will" focuses on the possibility of a future action or state.

3. A verb that occurs with 可能 *kěnéng* "possibly," 会 *huì* "will," or 可能会 *kěnéng huì* "possibly will" and is marked by 在 *zài* focuses on the duration or continuation of a future action.

4. A verb that occurs with 可能 *kěnéng* "possibly," 会 *huì* "will," or 可能会 *kěnéng huì* "possibly will" and is marked by 着 *zhe* focuses on the duration or continuation of a future state.

Other Future Forms

1. Immediate future: 快要 … 了 *kuàiyào … le*

   快要 *kuàiyào* is placed before the verb, and 了 *le* is added at the end of the sentence.

   快要下雨了。
   Kuàiyào xiàyǔ le.
   It is about to rain.

   NOTE An alternative form is 快 … 了 *kuài … le.*

2. Immediate future: 要 … 了

   要 *yào* is placed before the verb, and 了 *le* is added at the end of the sentence.

   明天**要开学了。**
   *Míngtiān **yào kāixué le**.*
   School is going to start tomorrow.

   NOTE An alternative form is 就要 … 了 *jiùyào … le.*

The difference between these two types of immediate future is that a time phrase may be included in No. 2, but not in No. 1.

English Conditional tense

Definition Many grammarians do not consider the conditional to be a true tense, but rather a mood. We consider it a tense here, however.

Forms The **conditional tense** is formed with the auxiliary verb *would* plus the infinitive of the main verb.

	SINGULAR	PLURAL
FIRST PERSON	*I would sing*	*we would sing*
SECOND PERSON	*you would sing*	*you would sing*
THIRD PERSON	*he/she would sing*	*they would sing*

The **conditional progressive tense** is formed with the conditional of the verb *to be* plus the present participle. It therefore requires three words.

	SINGULAR	PLURAL
FIRST PERSON	*I would be singing*	*we would be singing*
SECOND PERSON	*you would be singing*	*you would be singing*
THIRD PERSON	*he/she would be singing*	*they would be singing*

Would is often contracted to *'d*.

> *I'd go if you did.*

Uses The conditional is used

1. in Type 2 conditional sentences (*If* CONDITION, *(then)* RESULT.). (See the **Quick Check** on page 120.)

   > *If I were rich, (then) I **would go** to China every year.*

2. to convey the future from a past perspective.

FUTURE	*On Sunday, John said, "OK, I **will** see you on Monday."*
CONDITIONAL	*On Tuesday, Robert says, "John said that he **would** see us on Monday."*

Chinese Conditional sentences

Forms   The following chart shows the elements of conditional sentences in Chinese.

if CLAUSE	RESULT CLAUSE
要是 *yàoshi* + Subject + Predicate	Subject + 就 *jiù* + Predicate
如果 *rúguǒ* + Subject + Predicate	Subject + ∅ + Predicate
∅ + Subject + Predicate	

Conditional sentences consist of an *if* clause and a result clause. The *if* clause may contain a conjunction that has an "if" meaning, such as 要是 *yàoshi* or 如果 *rúguǒ,* or an "if" meaning may be implied but not expressed. Similarly, the result clause may contain a conjunction, such as 就 *jiù* "then," or the "result" meaning may be implied but not expressed.

The verbs in both the *if* and result clauses remain invariable, as they do in present, past, and future events; they are no different from verbs in nonconditional sentences. Therefore, how a conditional is interpreted (that is, whether it corresponds to the type 1, 2, or 3 conditional in English) depends on the context. The result clause sometimes contains an auxiliary verb or adverb expressing possibility, such as 会 *huì* "will," 可以 *kěyǐ* "may," or 一定 *yídìng* "certainly."

> 要是你准备好了，我们就走。
> *Yàoshi nǐ zhǔnbèi hǎo le, wǒmen jiù zǒu.*
> If you are ready, we will go.

> 天气凉快一点儿，我们就不用开空调了。
> *Tiānqì liángkuài yì diǎnr, wǒmen jiù búyòng kāi kōngtiáo le.*
> If the weather were cooler, we wouldn't need the air conditioning.

> 如果你那天在家，我一定会请你的。
> *Rúguǒ nǐ nà tiān zài jiā, wǒ yídìng huì qǐng nǐ de.*
> If you had been home that day, I would certainly have invited you.

Uses   A conditional sentence is used to describe the condition for an action to take place or a state to exist, and what the possible action or state is.

Word order

The *if* clause always precedes the result clause in Chinese. In a conditional sentence where neither the *if* nor the result word is expressed, the relation between the two clauses is still clear.

> 你去，我一定去。
> *Nǐ qù, wǒ yídìng qù.*
> If you go, I will definitely go.

Both the *if* word (要是 *yàoshi* or 如果 *rúguǒ*) and the result word (就 *jiù*) precede the verb in their clauses. The *if* word may occur before or after the subject of its clause, while the result word always occurs after the subject of its clause. Compare the following example with the one above.

> 你要是准备好了，我们就走。
> *Nǐ yàoshi zhǔnbèi hǎo le, wǒmen jiù zǒu.*
> If you are ready, we will go.

English Perfect (compound) tenses

Definition   The perfect tenses express

1. the time of the action or state.

2. the fact that it is completed.

"Perfect" in this sense comes from Latin *perfectus,* meaning "finished" or "completed." If something has been perfected, it needs no further work. "Perfect" here, then, does not mean "ideal."

Types   There are four perfect tenses corresponding to each of the tenses already discussed: present, past, future, and conditional.

English Present perfect tense

Forms   The present perfect tense is formed with the present tense of the verb *to have* plus the past participle of the main verb.

	SINGULAR	PLURAL
FIRST PERSON	*I have sung*	*we have sung*
SECOND PERSON	*you have sung*	*you have sung*
THIRD PERSON	*he/she has sung*	*they have sung*

CONTINUED ON PAGE 106 ▶

Completion by the present time

Forms The following chart shows the patterns used to express completion by the present time.

	COMPLETION OF A PARTICULAR ACTION	HAVING THE EXPERIENCE OF DOING SOMETHING
过 … 了 guò … le	Verb + 过 guò (+ Object) + 了 le	Verb + 过 guò (+ Object)
了 … 了 le … le	Verb + 了 le + Object + 了 le	
	Verb + 了 le + Duration phrase + 了 le	
Verb compound … 了 le	Verb–完 wán (+ Object) + 了 le	
	Verb–好 hǎo (+ Object) + 了 le	

NOTE 完 wán and 好 hǎo are resultative complements, attached to verbs to indicate the conclusion or result of an action.

1. Completion marked with 过 guò is of two types, depending on whether the action is a particular one or whether it relates to past experience (and may have happened on multiple occasions).

    a. Completion of a particular action is expressed by the verb plus the perfective marker 过 guò and the sentence-final particle 了 le.

    你吃过饭了吗？
    Nǐ chī guò fàn le ma?
    Have you **eaten**?

    我看过那个电影了。
    Wǒ kàn guò nà ge diànyǐng le.
    I **have seen** that movie.

    b. Having the experience of doing something is expressed by the verb plus the perfective marker 过 guò, but without the sentence-final particle 了 le.

    你去过中国吗？
    Nǐ qù guò Zhōngguó ma?
    Have you **been** to China?

    我以前见过那个人。
    Wǒ yǐqián jiàn guò nà ge rén.
    I **have seen** that man before.

2. Completion marked with 了 … 了 le … le is expressed by the verb plus the perfective marker 了 le and the sentence-final particle 了 le.

    我看了那本书了。
    Wǒ kàn le nà běn shū le.
    I **have read** that book.

    小王走了三天了。
    Xiǎo Wáng zǒu le sǎn tiān le.
    Xiao Wang **has been gone** for three days.

    NOTE 了 le occurs in two positions in a sentence: immediately after the verb and at the end of the sentence. In the postverbal position, it functions as a perfective marker, signaling that an event is viewed as a whole, including its beginning and end, as in "reading an entire book." (See page 95 for more examples.) In the sentence-final position, 了 le signals a change of state that is relevant to the reference time (present, past, or future) of the sentence, as in "at the present time, I have finished with the book." (See pages 101 and 107 for more examples.)

CONTINUED ON PAGE 107 ▶

Uses   This tense indicates that from the point of view of the present time, the action has been completed. Compare the following sentences.

> I **saw** *that movie yesterday.*
> I **have seen** *that movie.*

The first sentence, using *saw,* stresses a *past* action—what I did yesterday. The second stresses that I am currently experienced with that movie: I now know what it is about, that is, I *have* (present) *seen* (completed, finished with) that movie.

An idiomatic use of this tense is associated with the words *for* and *since.*

> I **have tried for** *three hours to phone him.*
> I **have tried since** *five o'clock to phone him.*

In the first sentence, the present perfect tense implies that there is a momentary lull, but the three hours of trying have lasted up to the present.

3. Completion marked with Verb compound ···了 *le* is expressed by a resultative compound verb whose second verbal element indicates result (for example, 完 *wán* "finished" or 好 *hǎo* "completed") plus the sentence-final particle 了 *le*.

他**写完**那封信了。
*Tā **xiě wán** nà fēng xìn **le**.*
He **has finished writing** that letter.

老师**讲完**那个故事了。
*Lǎoshī **jiǎng wán** nà ge gùshi **le**.*
The teacher **has finished telling** that story.

妈妈**洗好**那些脏衣服了。
*Māma **xǐ hǎo** nà xiē zāng yīfu **le**.*
Mom **has finished washing** those dirty clothes.

Uses The three patterns described above are used in a way similar to the present perfect tense in English.

1. Pattern 1 focuses on an event being completed by the present time.

2. Pattern 2 allows for a duration phrase. If one is present, the focus is on the duration after completion of an action. Otherwise, pattern 2 is similar to pattern 1.

3. Pattern 3 focuses on an action that requires a process before reaching completion, but the time of the process cannot be expressed.

English — Present perfect progressive tense

Definition   All progressive tenses emphasize duration, and all are conjugated with the auxiliary verb *to be* plus the present participle of the main verb.

Forms   The present perfect progressive tense in English uses *to be* in the present perfect with the main verb expressed by its present participle.

	SINGULAR	PLURAL
FIRST PERSON	*I have been singing*	*we have been singing*
SECOND PERSON	*you have been singing*	*you have been singing*
THIRD PERSON	*he/she has been singing*	*they have been singing*

Uses   Like other progressive tenses, the present perfect progressive tense emphasizes duration. Consider the following sentences.

> *I **have tried** since five o'clock to phone him.*
> *I **have been trying** for three hours to phone him.*

The second sentence stresses how long the three hours have seemed to me.

Chinese — Continuation from past to present

Forms   There are two major ways to express continuation: focusing on the continuation of an action or state, and focusing on the duration of time of an action or state.

1. **Focus on continuation**

    ACTION   (Duration phrase +) 一直 *yìzhí* + 在 *zài* + Verb

    STATE   (Duration phrase +) 一直 *yìzhí* + Verb + 着 *zhe*
    (Duration phrase +) 一直 *yìzhí* + Verb

2. **Focus on duration of time**

    INTRANSITIVE VERBS   Subject (+ 已经 *yǐjīng*) + Verb + 了 *le* + Duration phrase + 了 *le*

    TRANSITIVE VERBS   Subject + Verb + Object (+ 已经 *yǐjīng*) + Repeated Verb + 了 *le* + Duration phrase + 了 *le*
    Object + Subject (+ 已经 *yǐjīng*) + Verb + 了 *le* + Duration phrase + 了 *le*

CONTINUED ON PAGE 109 ▶

1. **Focus on continuation**

   a. **Continuation of an action**. 一直 *yìzhí* "continuously" and the progressive marker 在 *zài* are placed before the verb.

      Duration phrase + 　　一直 + 在 + Verb

      他 从下午到现在 　　一直 在 做 功课。
      Tā cóng xiàwǔ dào xiànzài **yìzhí zài zuò** *gōngkè.*
      He **has been doing** homework since this afternoon.

   b. **Continuation of a state**. 一直 *yìzhí* "continuously" is placed before the verb and the durative marker 着 *zhe* is placed after the verb.

      Duration phrase + 　　一直 + Verb + 着

      自从他离开以后， 我 就 一直 想 着 他。
      Zì cóng tā líkāi yǐhòu, wǒ jiù **yìzhí xiǎng zhe** *tā.*
      Since he left, I **have been thinking** of him.

      　　一直 + 　　Verb

      王先生 　　一直 跟他 保持 联系。
      Wáng xiānsheng **yìzhí** *gēn tā* **bǎochí** *liánxì.*
      Mr. Wang **has been keeping in touch** with him.

2. **Focus on duration of time**

   a. **Intransitive verbs**. If the verb is intransitive, it is followed by the perfective marker 了 *le*, the duration phrase, and the sentence-final particle 了 *le*.

      Subject + 已经 + Verb + 了 + Duration phrase + 了

      我 已经 等 了 三天 了。
      Wǒ **yǐjīng děng** *le* **sān tiān** *le.*
      I **have** already **been waiting for three days**.

   b. **Transitive verbs**. If the verb is transitive, the verb-object sequence is placed before the pattern for intransitive verbs; that is, the verb is repeated if it is transitive.

      Subject + Verb + Object + 　Repeated Verb + 了 + Duration phrase + 了

      我 开 那辆车 开 了 五年 了。
      Wǒ **kāi** *nà liàng chē* **kāi** *le* **wǔ nián** *le.*
      I **have been driving that car for five years**.

      Alternatively, to avoid repeating the verb, the object is placed before the subject.

      Object + 　Subject + Verb + 了 + Duration phrase + 了

      那辆车 我 开 了 五年 了。
      Nà liàng chē wǒ **kāi** *le* **wǔ nián** *le.*
      I **have been driving that car for five years**.

Uses These patterns express the continuation of an action or state from the past to the present, or how long the action or state has been going on between the past and the present.

Word order

The duration phrase occurs in different positions in the two patterns. In the first pattern, which focuses on continuation, the phrase indicating the duration of time occurs before the verb and the adverb 一直 *yìzhí* "continuously." In the second pattern, which focuses on the duration of time, the duration phrase occurs after the verb and immediately after the perfective marker 了 *le*.

English — Past perfect tense

Definition The past perfect tense indicates that some action (or state) was completed before some other past action (or state).

Forms The past perfect tense is formed with the simple past tense of the auxiliary verb *to have* plus the past participle of the main verb.

	SINGULAR	PLURAL
FIRST PERSON	*I had sung*	*we had sung*
SECOND PERSON	*you had sung*	*you had sung*
THIRD PERSON	*he/she had sung*	*they had sung*

These forms are often contracted to *I'd, you'd,* and so on.

*I'd **returned** the book before you asked for it.*

Uses Think of the past time sequence in terms of "yesterday" (past) and "last week" (further in the past).

*Mary **had finished** her homework before I **began** to talk to her.*
PAST PERFECT: last week   PAST: yesterday

Forms   The following chart shows the patterns used to express completion in the past.

COMPLETION IN THE PAST

过 … 了 *guò … le*	已经 *yǐjīng* + Verb + 过 *guò* (+ Object) + 了 *le*
了 … 了 *le … le*	已经 *yǐjīng* + Verb + 了 *le* + Object + 了 *le*
	已经 *yǐjīng* + Verb + 了 *le* + Duration phrase + 了 *le*
Verb compound … 了 *le*	已经 *yǐjīng* + Verb–完 *wán* (+ Object) + 了 *le*
	已经 *yǐjīng* + Verb–好 *hǎo* (+ Object) + 了 *le*

1. Completion marked with 过 … 了 *guò … le* is expressed by three elements: the adverb 已经 *yǐjīng* "already," which is placed before the verb; the perfective marker 过 *guò*, which is placed immediately after the verb; and the sentence-final particle 了 *le*. The portion of Verb + 过 (+ Object) + 了 is the same as Pattern 1 of "Completion by the present time" (see page 107).

   他来的时候，我已经吃过饭了。
   *Tā lái de shíhou, wǒ **yǐjīng chī guò** fàn **le**.*
   When he came, I **had already eaten**.

   你问我的时候，我已经看过那个电影了。
   *Nǐ wèn wǒ de shíhou, wǒ **yǐjīng kàn guò** nà ge diànyǐng **le**.*
   When you asked me, I **had already seen** that movie.

2. Completion marked with 了 … 了 *le … le* is also expressed by three elements: 已经 *yǐjīng* "already," the perfective marker 了 *le*, and the sentence-final particle 了 *le*.

   你问我要以前，我已经还了那本书了。
   *Nǐ wèn wǒ yào yǐqián, wǒ **yǐjīng huán le** nà běn shū **le**.*
   Before you asked me, I **had already returned** the book.

   他到的时候，小王已经走了三天了。
   *Tā dào de shíhou, Xiǎo Wáng **yǐjīng zǒu le** sǎn tiān **le**.*
   When he arrived, Xiao Wang **had already been gone** for three days.

3. Completion marked by Verb compound … 了 *le* is expressed by 已经 *yǐjīng* "already," a resultative compound verb, and the sentence-final particle 了 *le*.

   晚饭以前，他已经写完那封信了。
   *Wǎnfàn yǐqián, tā **yǐjīng xiě wán** nà fēng xìn **le**.*
   Before dinner, he **had already finished writing** that letter.

   钟响以前，老师已经讲完那个故事了。
   *Zhōng xiǎng yǐqián, lǎoshī **yǐjīng jiǎng wán** nà ge gùshi **le**.*
   Before the bell rang, the teacher **had already finished telling** that story.

Uses   These patterns are used in a way similar to the past perfect tense in English.

1. Pattern 1 focuses on an event being completed before a time in the past.

2. Pattern 2 allows for a duration phrase. If one is present, the focus is on the duration after completion of an action. Otherwise, pattern 2 is similar to pattern 1.

3. Pattern 3 focuses on an action that requires a process before reaching completion, but without the time of the process being expressed.

English Past perfect progressive tense

Definition This tense shares characteristics with others that have been introduced. It is

1. past (in terms of time).

2. perfect (in the sense of "completed").

3. progressive (with stress on duration).

Forms The past perfect progressive tense is formed with the past perfect tense of the verb *to be* plus the present participle of the main verb.

	SINGULAR	PLURAL
FIRST PERSON	*I had been singing*	*we had been singing*
SECOND PERSON	*you had been singing*	*you had been singing*
THIRD PERSON	*he/she had been singing*	*they had been singing*

CONTINUED ON PAGE 114 ▶

⨳⨳⨳⨳⨳ Continuation from past to past

Forms There are two major ways to express continuation: focusing on the continuation of an action or state, and focusing on the duration of time of an action or state.

1. Focus on continuation

ACTION   Time phrase + 一直 *yìzhí* + 在 *zài* + Verb

STATE   Time phrase + 一直 *yìzhí* + Verb + 着 *zhe*
Time phrase + 一直 *yìzhí* + Verb

2. Focus on duration of time

INTRANSITIVE VERBS   Time phrase + Subject + 已经 *yǐjīng* + Verb + 了 *le*
+ Duration phrase + 了 *le*

TRANSITIVE VERBS   Time phrase + Subject + Verb + Object + 已经 *yǐjīng*
+ Repeated Verb + 了 *le* + Duration phrase + 了 *le*
Time phrase + Object + Subject + 已经 *yǐjīng* + Verb
+ 了 *le* + Duration phrase + 了 *le*

Note the similarity to the constructions for expressing continuation from past to present (see page 108).

1. Focus on continuation

a. **Continuation of an action.** 一直 *yìzhí* "continuously" and the progressive marker 在 *zài* are placed before the verb.

Time phrase +   一直 + 在 + Verb

你来以前,   他 一直　在　做　功课。
*Nǐ lái yǐqián,   tā **yìzhí   zài   zuò** gōngkè.*
He **had been doing** homework before you came.

b. **Continuation of a state.** 一直 *yìzhí* "continuously" is placed before the verb and the durative marker 着 *zhe* is placed after the verb.

Time phrase +   一直 + Verb + 着

收到他的信以前,   我 一直　想　　着 他。
*Shōudào tā de xìn yǐqián, wǒ **yìzhí   xiǎng   zhe** tā.*
Before I received his letter, I **had been thinking** of him.

Time phrase +   一直 +   Verb

毕业以前, 小王   一直   跟他 保持　联系。
*Bìyè yǐqián, Xiǎo Wáng **yìzhí   gēn tā bǎochí** liánxì.*
Before graduating, Xiao Wang **had been keeping in touch** with him.

CONTINUED ON PAGE 115 ▶

Uses This tense expresses an action (or state) that had been continuing just before another past action (or state).

> *I **had been waiting** for three weeks when the letter **arrived**.*

That is, the wait started three weeks before the letter arrived.

2. **Focus on duration of time**

   a. **Intransitive verbs.** If the verb is intransitive, it is followed by the perfective marker 了 *le*, the duration phrase, and the sentence-final particle 了 *le*.

   Time phrase +   Subject + 已经 + Verb + 了 + Duration phrase + 了

   信寄到的时候，   我   已经   等   了   三天   了。

   Xìn jì dào de shíhou,   *wǒ*   ***yǐjīng děng le sān tiān***   *le.*

   When the letter arrived, I **had already been waiting for three days**.

   b. **Transitive verbs.** If the verb is transitive, the verb-object sequence is placed before the pattern for intransitive verbs; that is, the verb is repeated if it is transitive.

   Time phrase + Subject + Verb + Object +   已经 + Repeated Verb + 了

   毕业的时候，我   开   那辆车   已经   开   了

   Bìyè de shíhou,   *wǒ*   *kāi*   *nà liàng chē yǐjīng kāi*   *le*

       + Duration phrase + 了

       五年   了。

       wǔ nián   *le.*

   When I graduated, I **had already been driving that car for five years**.

   Alternatively, to avoid repeating the verb, the object is placed before the subject.

   Time phrase + Object +   Subject + 已经 + Verb + 了 + Duration phrase + 了

   毕业的时候，那辆车   我   已经   开   了   五年   了。

   Bìyè de shíhou, ***nà liàng chē*** *wǒ*   ***yǐjīng kāi le wǔ nián***   *le.*

   When I graduated, I **had already been driving that car for five years**.

Uses The patterns described above express the continuation of an action or state from a time in the past to another time in the past, or how long the action or state lasted between the two times in the past.

Word order

There are usually two time phrases in one of these sentences: a phrase referring to a time in the past and a phrase signaling the duration. The former occurs before the verb, often at the beginning of the sentence, whereas the duration phrase occurs after the verb.

English Future perfect tense

Definition   This tense expresses an action that will be completed at some time in the future.

Forms   The future perfect tense is formed with the future tense of the auxiliary *to have* plus the past participle of the main verb.

	SINGULAR	PLURAL
FIRST PERSON	*I will have sung*	*we will have sung*
SECOND PERSON	*you will have sung*	*you will have sung*
THIRD PERSON	*he/she will have sung*	*they will have sung*

These forms are often contracted in speech to *I'll've, you'll've,* and so on.

Uses   This tense is used to express future completion.

I **will have finished** the book before the professor **gives** an exam.
FUTURE PERFECT   PRESENT

In the second clause, the present tense is used in English, even though the verb refers to an action in the future; the professor is not giving an exam now.

Forms Completion in the future uses the same patterns as completion in the past. The difference in meaning is conveyed by the context. An auxiliary verb or adverb indicating possibility, such as 会 *huì* "will" or 可能 *kěnéng* "maybe," is sometimes present.

The following chart shows the patterns used to express completion in the future.

COMPLETION IN THE FUTURE

过 … 了 *guò … le*	(会 *huì* +) 已经 *yǐjīng* + Verb + 过 *guò* (+ Object) + 了 *le*
了 … 了 *le … le*	(会 *huì* +) 已经 *yǐjīng* + Verb + 了 *le* + Object + 了 *le*
	(会 *huì* +) 已经 *yǐjīng* + Verb + 了 *le* + Duration phrase + 了 *le*
Verb compound … 了 *le*	(会 *huì* +) 已经 *yǐjīng* + Verb-完 *wán* (+ Object) + 了 *le*
	(会 *huì* +) 已经 *yǐjīng* + Verb-好 *hǎo* (+ Object) + 了 *le*

1. Completion marked with 过 … 了 *guò … le* is expressed by three elements: the adverb 已经 *yǐjīng* "already," which is placed before the verb; the perfective marker 过 *guò*, which is placed immediately after the verb; and the sentence-final particle 了 *le*. The portion of Verb + 过 (+ Object) + 了 is the same as Pattern 1 of "Completion by the present time" (see page 107).

    等你来的时候，我**可能已经吃过饭了**。
    *Děng nǐ lái de shíhou, wǒ **kěnéng yǐjīng chī guò fàn le**.*
    When you come later, **maybe I will have already eaten**.

2. Completion marked with 了 … 了 *le … le* is also expressed by three elements: 已经 *yǐjīng* "already," the perfective marker 了 *le*, and the sentence-final particle 了 *le*.

    等你到的时候，小王**可能已经走了**三天了。
    *Děng nǐ dào de shíhou, Xiǎo Wáng **kěnéng yǐjīng zǒu le** sǎn tiān **le**.*
    By the time you arrive, Xiao Wang **may have already been gone** for three days.

3. Completion marked by Verb compound … 了 *le* is expressed by 已经 *yǐjīng* "already," a resultative compound verb, and the sentence-final particle 了 *le*.

    老师考试以前，我**会已经读完**这本书了。
    *Lǎoshī kǎoshì yǐqián, wǒ **huì yǐjīng dú wán** zhè běn shū **le**.*
    Before the teacher gives an exam, I **will have already finished reading** the book.

Uses The three patterns described above are used in a way similar to the future perfect tense in English.

1. Pattern 1 focuses on an event being completed before a time in the future.

2. Pattern 2 allows for a duration phrase. If one is present, the focus is on the duration. Otherwise, pattern 2 is similar to pattern 1.

3. Pattern 3 focuses on an action that requires a process before reaching completion, but without the time of the process being expressed.

✓ *QUICK CHECK*

The three types of completion—(1) completion by the present time, (2) completion in the past, and (3) completion in the future—share the same basic forms.

过 … 了 *guò … le*	Verb + 过 *guò* + (Object) + 了 *le*
了 … 了 *le … le*	Verb + 了 *le* + Object + 了 *le*
	Verb + 了 *le* + Duration phrase + 了 *le*
Verb compound … 了 *le*	Verb + 完 *wán* + (Object) + 了 *le*
	Verb + 好 *hǎo* + (Object) + 了 *le*

Types (2) and (3) almost always occur with 已经 *yǐjīng* "already"; type (3) may also occur with 会 *huì* "will" or 可能 *kěnéng* "maybe."

English Future perfect progressive tense

Definition   This tense expresses an action or state that will be continued and then completed in the future.

Forms   The future perfect progressive tense is formed with the future perfect tense of the auxiliary *to be* plus the present participle of the main verb.

	SINGULAR	PLURAL
FIRST PERSON	*I will have been singing*	*we will have been singing*
SECOND PERSON	*you will have been singing*	*you will have been singing*
THIRD PERSON	*he/she will have been singing*	*they will have been singing*

Uses   This tense is used to emphasize the duration of an action whose beginning point is not specified but whose completion (at least provisionally) will be in the future.

> I **will have been studying** English for 16 years when I **graduate**.
> FUTURE PERFECT PROGRESSIVE   PRESENT

Although graduation is in the future, English uses the present tense. The sentence does not indicate when the speaker will graduate, nor when he or she began to study English. The important point is the relationship between the verbs in the two clauses; 16 years of study will be completed at the moment in the future when I graduate.

Chinese Continuation from past to future

Forms   Unlike continuation from past to present and from past to past, there is only one way to express continuation from past to future: focusing on the duration of the action or state. The conjunction 就 *jiù* "then" is often present to give the sense that the duration is lengthy.

INTRANSITIVE VERBS   Time phrase + Subject (+ 就 *jiù*) + 已经 *yǐjīng* + Verb + 了 *le* + Duration phrase + 了 *le*

TRANSITIVE VERBS   Time phrase + Subject + Verb + Object (+ 就 *jiù*) + 已经 *yǐjīng* + Repeated Verb + 了 *le* + Duration phrase + 了 *le*

Time phrase + Object + Subject (+ 就 *jiù*) + 已经 *yǐjīng* + Verb + 了 *le* + Duration phrase + 了 *le*

CONTINUED ON PAGE 119 ▶

1. **Intransitive verbs.** If the verb is intransitive, it is followed by the perfective marker 了 *le*, the duration phrase, and the sentence-final particle 了 *le*.

Time phrase +   Subject + 就 + 已经 + Verb + 了

等信寄到的时候,   我   就   已经   等   了

Děng xìn jì dào de shíhou, wǒ   *jiù*   *yǐjīng*   *děng*   *le*

    + Duration phrase + 了

三天   了。

sān tiān   **le.**

When the letter arrives, I **will have already been waiting for three days.**

2. **Transitive verbs.** If the verb is transitive, the verb-object sequence is placed before the pattern for intransitive verbs; that is, the verb is repeated if it is transitive.

Time phrase +   Subject + Verb + Object +   就 + 已经

等明年毕业的时候,   我   开   那辆车   就   已经

Děng míngnián bìyè de shíhou, wǒ   *kāi*   *nà liàng chē jiù*   *yǐjīng*

    + Repeated Verb + 了 + Duration phrase + 了

开   了   五年   了。

kāi   **le**   **wǔ nián**   **le.**

By the time I graduate next year, I **will have already been driving that car for five years.**

Alternatively, to avoid repeating the verb, the object is placed before the subject.

Time phrase +   Object +   Subject + 就 + 已经 + Verb

等明年毕业的时候,   那辆车   我   就   已经   开

Děng míngnián bìyè de shíhou, nà liàng chē wǒ   *jiù*   *yǐjīng*   *kāi*

    + 了 + Duration phrase + 了

了   五年   了。

le   **wǔ nián**   **le.**

When I graduate next year, I **will have already been driving that car for five years.**

Uses   The patterns described above express the continuation of an action or state from an unspecified time in the past to a time in the future, or how long the action or state lasts between the two points in time.

☑ QUICK CHECK

	FOCUS ON CONTINUATION (NONSTOP)	FOCUS ON DURATION (HOW LONG)
Continuation from past to present	一直 *yìzhí* + 在 *zài* + Verb 一直 *yìzhí* + Verb + 着 *zhe* 一直 *yìzhí* + Verb	Verb + 了 *le* + Duration + 了 *le*
Continuation from past to past	一直 *yìzhí* + 在 *zài* + Verb 一直 *yìzhí* + Verb + 着 *zhe* 一直 *yìzhí* + Verb	已经 *yǐjīng* + Verb + 了 *le* + Duration phrase + 了 *le*
Continuation from past to future		(会 *huì*) + 已经 *yǐjīng* + Verb + 了 *le* + Duration + 了 *le*

English Perfect conditional tense

Forms
This tense is formed with the conditional tense of *to have* plus the past participle of the main verb.

	SINGULAR	PLURAL
FIRST PERSON	*I would have sung*	*we would have sung*
SECOND PERSON	*you would have sung*	*you would have sung*
THIRD PERSON	*he/she would have sung*	*they would have sung*

These forms are often contracted in speech to *I'd've, you'd've,* and so on.

> **I'd've** *come if I'd known.*

Uses
This tense is used primarily in the result clauses of Type 3 conditional sentences (see the **Quick Check** below).

> He **would have seen** *the film if he* **had known** *that it was so good.*
> We **would have come** *if we* **had known** *about it.*
>   PERFECT CONDITIONAL   PAST PERFECT

The *'d* in English can be a contraction of both *had* and *would*. This can cause some confusion unless the meaning of a sentence is analyzed.

> *If he'***d said** *he needed it, I'***d have given** *it to him.*
>   PLUPERFECT   PERFECT CONDITIONAL

 **QUICK CHECK**

THE THREE MOST COMMON TYPES OF CONDITIONAL SENTENCES IN ENGLISH

if CLAUSE	RESULT CLAUSE	*if* CLAUSE	RESULT CLAUSE
1. *If you* **are** *ready,*	*we* **will** *go.*	PRESENT	FUTURE
2. *If you* **were** *ready,*	*we* **would** *go.*	SUBJUNCTIVE	CONDITIONAL
3. *If you* **had been** *ready,*	*we* **would have** *gone.*	PAST PERFECT	PERFECT CONDITIONAL

English Perfect conditional progressive tense

Forms
This tense is formed with the perfect conditional tense of the auxiliary *to be* plus the present participle of the main verb.

	SINGULAR	PLURAL
FIRST PERSON	*I would have been singing*	*we would have been singing*
SECOND PERSON	*you would have been singing*	*you would have been singing*
THIRD PERSON	*he/she would have been singing*	*they would have been singing*

Uses
The perfect conditional progressive tense is used in the same way as the perfect conditional, except that the idea of duration is added.

> I **would** *not* **have been sleeping** *when you arrived, if I* **had known** *you were coming.*
>   PERFECT CONDITIONAL PROGRESSIVE   PAST PERFECT

Chinese Perfect conditional sentences

For conditional sentences in Chinese, see page 103.

Definition The passive voice is used when the subject receives the action of the verb.

ACTIVE VOICE	**The dog**	*bit*	**Susie.**
	SUBJECT	ACTIVE VERB	DIRECT OBJECT
PASSIVE VOICE	**Susie**	*was bitten*	*by the dog.*
	SUBJECT	PASSIVE VERB	AGENT

Notice that the direct object of the active verb becomes the subject of the passive verb. The active verb's subject is placed after the passive verb in a prepositional phrase and is called the agent. It is not always expressed, as in the colloquial *John got caught*; for such a sentence, it is either not important or not known by whom or what John was caught.

Forms The passive voice is formed with *to be* or *to get* plus the past participle of the main verb.

Only transitive verbs (ones that have a direct object) can be made passive.

PRESENT	ACTIVE	John **catches** the ball.
	PASSIVE	The ball **is caught** by John.
PAST	ACTIVE	The man **read** the book.
	PASSIVE	The book **was read** by the man.
FUTURE	ACTIVE	Mrs. Smith **will lead** the discussion.
	PASSIVE	The discussion **will be led** by Mrs. Smith.
PERFECT CONDITIONAL	ACTIVE	The class **would have finished** the job, but . . .
	PASSIVE	The job **would have been finished** by the class, but . . .

All the perfect and progressive tenses of the passive voice are formed in the same way. Some forms can be very long and are seldom used; an example of the passive future perfect progressive follows.

*The work **will have been being done** at 3 PM.*

Chinese Passive voice

Forms The most common passive voice construction in Chinese is with 被 *bèi*. This construction has both a long and a short form.

LONG FORM

ACTIVE VOICE

SUBJECT	VERB	DIRECT OBJECT
狗	咬了	苏茜。
Gǒu	*yǎo le*	*Sūxī.*
The dog	bit	**Susie.**

PASSIVE VOICE

SUBJECT	PASSIVE MARKER	AGENT	VERB
苏茜	被	狗	咬了。
Sūxī	*bèi*	*gǒu*	*yǎo le.*
Susie		**the dog**	bit

Susie was bitten by **the dog**.

CONTINUED ON PAGE 123 ▶

SHORT FORM

ACTIVE VOICE

SUBJECT	VERB	DIRECT OBJECT
狗	咬了	苏茜。
Gǒu	*yǎo le*	*Sūxī.*
The dog	bit	**Susie.**

PASSIVE VOICE

SUBJECT	PASSIVE MARKER	VERB
苏茜	被	咬了。
Sūxī	*bèi*	*yǎo le.*
Susie		bit

Susie was bitten.

In addition to being marked by 被 *bèi*, the passive can also be expressed with 叫 *jiào*, 让 *ràng*, and 给 *gěi*. The expressions 叫 *jiào* and 让 *ràng* have only a long form, while 给 *gěi* has both a long and a short form.

LONG FORM

SUBJECT	PASSIVE MARKER	AGENT	VERB
苏茜	叫 / 让 / 给	狗	咬了。
Sūxī	*jiào/ràng/gěi*	*gǒu*	*yǎo le.*
Susie		**the dog**	bit

Susie was bitten by **the dog**.

SHORT FORM

SUBJECT	PASSIVE MARKER	VERB
苏茜	给	咬了。
Sūxī	*gěi*	*yǎo le.*
Susie		bit

Susie was bitten.

Uses The passive voice is not commonly used in Chinese. First of all, not all active sentences can be turned into passive sentences. A sentence where the object is not affected usually does not have the passive form.

班上同学很喜欢玛丽。
Bānshang tóngxué hěn xǐhuan Mǎlì.
The students in class like Mary.

If the passive form is possible, it is often used to describe an unfavorable situation, as in the examples of dog biting above. A common alternative to the passive voice is to place the object before the verb and not mention the subject.

晚饭做好了。
Wǎnfàn zuò hǎo le.
Dinner is ready.

那辆车卖了一千块钱。
Nà liàng chē mài le yìqiān kuài qián.
The car was sold for a thousand dollars.

Such sentences are translated into English as passive sentences, but they are not considered passive sentences in Chinese.

 Imperative mood

Definition The imperative mood is the mood used to give commands.

Forms The forms of the English imperative are very similar to those of the present indicative, with a few exceptions.

The second-person imperative (both singular and plural) has only one form: *Sing!*

For the first-person plural, the auxiliary verb *let* is used.

> *Let's sing!*

For the third-person (singular and plural), the auxiliary verbs *let, have,* and *make* are used.

> *Let her sing!*
> *Have them come in!*
> *Make him stop!*

No subject is expressed in an imperative sentence.

IRREGULAR IMPERATIVES English has only one irregular imperative: for the verb *to be.* Compare the following sentences.

INDICATIVE	IMPERATIVE
You are good.	*Be good!*
We are quiet.	*Let's be quiet!*

Chinese Imperative mood

Forms The forms of the imperative are the same as those of the indicative, with two exceptions.

1. The second-person subject does not need to be expressed.

2. In negation, the negative form is 别 *bié* or 不要 *búyào* "don't."

SECOND PERSON

SINGULAR AND PLURAL	唱！ *Chàng!* Sing!
SINGULAR	你唱！ *Nǐ chàng!* You sing!
PLURAL	你们唱！ *Nǐmen chàng!* You sing!

CONTINUED ON PAGE 125 ▸

FIRST-PERSON PLURAL

我们来唱！

Wǒmen lái chàng!

Let's sing!

THIRD PERSON

SINGULAR

让他唱！

Ràng tā chàng!

Let him sing!

PLURAL

让他们唱！

Ràng tāmen chàng!

Let them sing!

Negative imperative

SECOND PERSON

SINGULAR AND PLURAL

别唱！

Bié chàng!

Don't sing!

SINGULAR

你别唱！

Nǐ bié chàng!

You don't sing!

PLURAL

你们别唱！

Nǐmen bié chàng!

You don't sing!

FIRST-PERSON PLURAL

我们别唱！

Wǒmen bié chàng!

Let's not sing!

THIRD PERSON

SINGULAR

让他别唱！

Ràng tā bié chàng!

Let him not sing!

PLURAL

让他们别唱！

Ràng tāmen bié chàng!

Let them not sing!

English Subjunctive mood

Definition   The subjunctive is the mood that expresses what may be true.

Forms   The **present subjunctive** (or the auxiliary verb in a compound tense) has the same form for all persons: the basic (infinitive) form of the verb. It is different from the indicative only for

1. the third-person singular.

   that he take
   that she have

2. the verb *to be.*

   PRESENT   *that I be, that he be*
   PAST   *that I were, that she were*

Uses   The subjunctive is rarely used in English. For that reason, it tends to be disregarded except in certain fixed expressions. Nevertheless, it does have some specific uses that are important in formal English.

1. In contrary-to-fact conditions

   *If I **were** you . . .*
   *"If this **be** madness, yet there is method in it." (Hamlet)*

2. After verbs like *wish, suppose, insist, urge, demand, ask, recommend,* and *suggest*

   *I wish that he **were** able to come.*
   *They insisted that we **be** present.*
   *I recommend that she **learn** the subjunctive.*

3. After some impersonal expressions, such as *it is necessary* and *it is important*

   *It is necessary that Mary **see** its importance.*
   *It is important that he **avoid** errors.*

4. In certain fixed expressions

   *So **be** it!*
   *Long **live** the Queen!*
   *Heaven **forbid**!*
   *Far **be** it from me to suggest that!*

   Most of these fixed expressions express a third-person imperative; the idea "I wish that" is implied, but not expressed.

   Except for the fixed expressions, English speakers tend to use an alternative expression whenever possible, usually with modal verbs (auxiliaries), to avoid the subjunctive in conversation and informal writing. Compare the following sentences with the examples above.

   *I wish that he **could come**.*
   *I told her that she **must learn** the subjunctive.*
   *It is important for him **to avoid** errors.*
   *Mary **needs to see** its importance.*

Chinese Subjunctive mood

Chinese does not have a subjunctive mood. Contrary-to-fact conditions are expressed in conditional sentences (see page 103). Other types of sentences that use the English subjunctive are expressed in the indicative mood in Chinese.

Exercises

The following exercises, grouped by part of speech, test your grasp of key grammatical aspects of Chinese. As a reminder of the similarities and differences between Chinese and English, a cross-reference is provided at the end of each exercise to the relevant grammar points discussed in this book. An answer key is provided after the appendices.

Nouns

A   *Add the correct measure word to each of the following Chinese nouns.*

1. 一 *yì* _____ 书 *shū* a book

2. 两 *liǎng* _____ 帽子 *màozi* two hats

3. 五 *wǔ* _____ 桌子 *zhuōzi* five tables

4. 三 *sān* _____ 衣服 *yīfu* three pieces of clothing

5. 一 *yì* _____ 巧克力 *qiǎokèlì* a box of chocolate

6. 两 *liǎng* _____ 橘子 *júzi* two tangerines

7. 四 *sì* _____ 学生 *xuésheng* four students

8. 一 *yí* _____ 家具 *jiājù* a suite of furniture

9. 五 *wǔ* _____ 牛 *niú* five cows

10. 两 *liǎng* _____ 树 *shù* two trees

   ◀ *For more help, see* Introducing determiners, *page 17, and* Appendix A, *page 145.*

B   *Add the correct determiner to each of the following Chinese nouns. Don't forget to include a measure word where necessary.*

1. _____ 牛奶 *niúnǎi* a lot of milk

2. _____ 人 *rén* a few people

3. _____ 照片 *zhàopiàn* every picture

4. _____ 面包 *miànbāo* some bread

5. _____ 老师 *lǎoshī* many teachers

6. _____ 椅子 *yǐzi* a few chairs

7. _____ 书 *shū* many books

8. _____ 苹果 *píngguǒ* some apples

9. _____ 雨 *yǔ* a lot of rain

10. _____ 狗 *gǒu* each dog

◀ *For more help, see* Introducing determiners, *page* 17.

Pronouns

A *Rewrite each of the following sentences, replacing the noun phrase in bold type with the correct pronoun.*

1. **李先生**是中国人。***Lǐ xiānsheng*** *shì Zhōngguó rén.*

   _____

2. **这位女士**住在纽约。***Zhè wèi nǚshì*** *zhù zài Niǔyuē.*

   _____

3. **小李和我**是好朋友。***Xiǎo Lǐ hé wǒ*** *shì hǎo péngyǒu.*

   _____

4. **我弟弟**喜欢**你妹妹**。***Wǒ dìdi*** *xǐhuan **nǐ mèimei**.*

   _____

5. **这辆车**有四扇门。***Zhè liàng chē*** *yǒu sì shàn mén.*

   _____

6. 我跟**一些朋友**出去了。*Wǒ gēn **yì xiē péngyǒu** chūqù le.*

   _____

7. 你要请**他姐姐**吃饭吗？*Nǐ yào qǐng **tā jiějie** chī fàn ma?*

   _____

8. 我看完**那本书**了。*Wǒ kànwán **nà běn shū** le.*

   _____

9. 他开走**那辆车**了。*Tā kāizǒu **nà liàng chē** le.*

   _____

10. 他在给**他爸爸**打电话。*Tā zài gěi **tā bàba** dǎ diànhuà.*

   _____

◀ *For more help, see* Personal pronouns, *page* 23.

B *Complete each of the following sentences with the missing pronoun.*

1. 这是你的书吗？ *Zhè shì nǐ de shū ma?*

   不，这是 ＿＿＿＿＿＿＿＿＿。 *Bù, zhè shì* ＿＿＿＿＿＿＿＿＿. (his)

2. 那辆红车是你的吗？ *Nà liàng hóng chē shì nǐ de ma?*

   对，是 ＿＿＿＿＿＿＿＿＿。 *Duì, shì* ＿＿＿＿＿＿＿＿＿. (mine)

3. 你在跟谁说话？ *Nǐ zài gēn shéi shuō huà?*

   我在跟 ＿＿＿＿＿＿＿＿＿ 说话。 *Wǒ zài gēn* ＿＿＿＿＿＿＿＿＿ *shuō huà.* (myself)

4. 我的房间比 ＿＿＿＿＿＿＿＿＿ 大。 *Wǒ de fángjiān bǐ* ＿＿＿＿＿＿＿＿＿ *dà.* (hers)

5. 小李忘了 ＿＿＿＿＿＿＿＿＿ 电话号码。 *Xiǎo Lǐ wang le* ＿＿＿＿＿＿＿＿＿ *diànhuà hàomǎ.* (his own)

6. 那只狗是谁的？ 是 ＿＿＿＿＿＿＿＿＿。 *Nà zhī gǒu shì shéi de? Shì* ＿＿＿＿＿＿＿＿＿. (ours)

7. 他从窗里看见 ＿＿＿＿＿＿＿＿＿。 *Tā cóng chuān lǐ kànjiàn* ＿＿＿＿＿＿＿＿＿. (himself)

8. 我的朋友们说他们会照顾 ＿＿＿＿＿＿＿＿＿。 *Wǒ de péngyǒumen shuō tāmen huì zhàogù* ＿＿＿＿＿＿＿＿＿. (themselves)

◀ *For more help, see* Personal pronouns, *page 23, and* Reflexive/reciprocal forms, *page 27.*

C *Complete each of the following Chinese sentences so that it matches the meaning of the English sentence.*

1. I like my bicycle, but he prefers his.

   我喜欢我的脚踏车，但是他喜欢 ＿＿＿＿＿＿＿＿＿。

   Wǒ xǐhuan wǒ de jiǎotàchē, dànshì tā xǐhuān ＿＿＿＿＿＿＿＿＿.

2. This house is older than ours.

   这个房子比 ＿＿＿＿＿＿＿＿＿ 旧。

   Zhè ge fángzi bǐ ＿＿＿＿＿＿＿＿＿ *jiù.*

3. These aren't Marie's books, they're mine.

   这不是玛丽的书，这是 ＿＿＿＿＿＿＿＿＿。

   Zhè bú shì Mǎlì de shū, zhè shì ＿＿＿＿＿＿＿＿＿.

4. I have my diskettes. Do you have yours?

   我有我的磁盘，你有 ＿＿＿＿＿＿＿＿＿ 吗？

   Wǒ yǒu wǒ de cípán, nǐ yǒu ＿＿＿＿＿＿＿＿＿ *ma?*

5. She needs to use my pencil, because she has lost hers.

   她需要用我的铅笔，因为她丢了 ＿＿＿＿＿＿＿＿＿。

   Tā xūyào yòng wǒ de qiānbǐ, yīnwèi tā diū le ＿＿＿＿＿＿＿＿＿.

6. My bicycle is broken. Can I use yours?

我的脚踏车坏了。我能不能用 _____?

Wǒ de jiǎotàchē huài le, wǒ néng bù nèng yòng _____?

7. I brought my photos, and they brought theirs.

我带来了我的照片，他们带来了_____。

Wǒ dàilái le wǒ de zhàopiàn, tāmen dàilái le _____.

8. Our dog is bigger than theirs.

我们的狗比 _____ 大。

Wǒmen de gǒu bǐ _____ *dà.*

◀ *For more help, see* Pronominal possessive forms, *page 25.*

D *Complete each of the following sentences with the information provided. Don't forget to insert the particle* 的 *de where required.*

1. 我看了这篇文章。*Wǒ kàn le zhè piān wénzhāng.*

这是我看 _____ 文章。*Zhè shì wǒ kàn* _____ *wénzhāng.*

2. 我以前在这个地方工作。*Wǒ yǐqián zài zhè ge dìfang gōngzuò.*

这是我 _____ 的地方。*Zhè shì wǒ* _____ *de dìfang.*

3. 这家餐馆在街口，非常有名。*Zhè jiā cānguǎn zài jiēkǒu, fēicháng yǒumíng.*

_____ 的这家餐馆 非常有名。_____ *de zhè jiā cānguǎn fēicháng yǒumíng.*

4. 你要什么？我们不知道。*Nǐ yào shénme? Wǒmen bù zhīdào.*

我们不知道你 _____ 是什么。*Wǒmen bù zhīdào nǐ*

_____ *shì shénme.*

5. 我在这家糕饼店买面包。*Wǒ zài zhè jiā gāobǐng diàn mǎi miànbāo.*

这是 _____ 的糕饼店。*Zhè shì* _____ *de gāobǐng diàn.*

6. 我们在那个地方开晚会。*Wǒmen zài nà ge dìfang kāi wǎnhuì.*

这是我们 _____ 地方。*Zhè shì wǒmen* _____ *dìfāng.*

7. 我对这个题目有兴趣。*Wǒ duì zhè ge tímù yǒu xìngqù.*

这是我 _____ 的题目。*Zhè shì wǒ* _____ *de tímù.*

8. 这个工程师我们认识，他的能力很强。*Zhè ge gōngchéngshī wǒmen rènshì, tā de nénglì hěn qiáng.*

_____ 的工程师能力很强。_____ *de gōngchéngshī nénglì hěn qiáng.*

◀ *For more help, see* Pronominal possessive forms, *page 25.*

E *Translate each of the following sentences into Chinese, using demonstrative pronouns and adjectives.*

1. This book is expensive; that one is inexpensive.

   _____

2. My house is on the east side of the town, (and) my younger sister's is on the west side.

   _____

3. These restaurants are good, but those are better.

   _____

4. She is the one he loves.

   _____

5. Do you want those pastries or these?

   _____

6. We can take (用 *yòng*) my car. Marie's is not big enough.

   _____

◀ *For more help, see* Demonstrative pronouns, *page 37, and* Demonstrative adjectives, *page 51.*

F *Complete each of the following Chinese sentences with the missing interrogative pronoun so that the Chinese sentence matches the meaning of the English sentence.*

1. Whom are you writing to?

   你在给 _____ 写信？

   Nǐ zài gěi _____ xiě xìn?

2. What are you looking for?

   你在找 _____ ？

   Nǐ zài zhǎo _____ ?

3. I like these two cars. Which is less expensive?

   我喜欢这两辆车。_____ 比较便宜？

   Wǒ xǐhuān zhè liǎng liàng chē. _____ bǐjiào piányi?

4. What is the child afraid of?

   这个小孩怕 _____ ？

   Zhè ge xiǎohái pà _____ ?

5. Whom is she going out with?

   她在跟 _____ 交往？

   Tā zài gēn _____ jiāowǎng?

6. What are you thinking about?

你在想 _____?

Nǐ zài xiǎng _____?

7. There are so many newspapers. Which ones do you read?

有那么多报纸，你看 _____?

Yǒu nàme duō bàozhǐ, nǐ kàn _____?

8. Who works there?

_____ 在那儿工作?

_____ *zài nàr gōngzuò?*

9. What did you do?

你做了_____?

Nǐ zuò le _____?

10. Whom did you see?

你看见 _____ 了?

Nǐ kànjiàn _____ le ?

11. What's happening?

发生了_____ 事?

Fāshēng le _____ shì?

12. Whom are these gifts for?

这些礼物是要给 _____ 的?

Zhè xiē lǐwù shì yào gěi _____ de?

◀ *For more help, see* Interrogative pronouns, *pages 39–40.*

Adjectives

A *Change each of the following simple adjectives to a reduplicated adjective.*

1. 高的 *gāo de* _____

2. 干净的 *gānjìng de* _____

3. 黑的 *hēi de* _____

4. 瘦的 *shòu de* _____

5. 高大的 *gāodà de* _____

6. 快乐的 *kuàilè de* _____

7. 清楚的 *qīngchu de* _____

8. 安静的 *ānjìng de* _____

◀ *For more help, see* Descriptive adjectives, *page 45.*

B *Translate each of the following sentences into Chinese.*

1. Xiaoming is more intelligent than Xiaohua.

   _____

2. My older sister is less happy than my older brother.

   _____

3. Mary is as old as Nancy.

   _____

4. It's the best book in the library.

   _____

5. The subway is faster than the bus.

   _____

6. He is the worst student in the class.

   _____

7. My course is less interesting than their course.

   _____

8. I am as tall as my father.

   _____

◀ *For more help, see* Comparison of adjectives, *page 47.*

C *Complete each the following sentences with the appropriate form of the demonstrative adjective. The answer may require a measure word.*

1. 你认识 _____ 人 (near [sing.]) 吗？

   Nǐ rènshi _____ rén ma?

2. _____ 看法 (near [pl.]) 很有意思。

   _____ kànfǎ hěn yǒu yìsi.

3. 你去 _____ 馆子 (far) 吃过吗？

   Nǐ qù _____ guǎnzi chī guò ma?

4. _____ 文章 (near [sing.]) 写得很好。

   _____ wénzhāng xiě de hěn hǎo.

5. _____ 女士 (far [sing.]) 是谁？

_____ *nǚshì shì shéi?*

6. _____ 学生 (near [pl.]) 很认真。

_____ *xuésheng hěn rènzhēn.*

7. _____ (far [pl.]) 公园很漂亮。

_____ *gōngyuán hěn piàoliang.*

8. _____ 学校 (far [sing.]) 很有名。

_____ *xuéxiào hěn yǒumíng.*

◀ *For more help, see* Demonstrative adjectives, *page 51. For a list of measure words, see* Appendix A, *page 145.*

D *Translate each of the following phrases into Chinese.*

1. her teacher _____

2. my house _____

3. his friends _____

4. our dog _____

5. their car _____

6. your Chinese _____

7. your [pl.] table _____

8. our cafeteria _____

◀ *For more help, see* Adjectival possessive forms, *page 53.*

E *Complete each of the following questions with the appropriate question word.*

1. 这是 _____ (whose) 书？

Zhè shì _____ shū?

2. _____ 学生 [pl.] 今天没来？

_____ *xuésheng jīntiān méi lái?*

3. _____ 是你最喜欢的课？

_____ *shì nǐ zuì xǐhuan de kè?*

4. 教室里有 _____ 东西？

Jiàoshì li yǒu _____ dōngxi?

5. 那只狗是 _____ (whose) 狗？

Nà zhī gǒu shì _____ gǒu?

6. 你在读 _____ (which) 书？

Nǐ zài dú _____ shū?

7. _____ 学生 [pl.] 是日本人?

   _____ xuésheng shì Rìběn rén?

8. 今天晚饭有 _____ 菜?

   Jīntiān wǎnfàn yǒu _____ cài?

9. 她从 _____ (which) 门进来?

   Tā cóng _____ mén jìn lái?

10. 你哥哥买了 _____ 车?

    Nǐ gēge mǎi le _____ chē?

◀ *For more help, see* Interrogative adjectives, *page 55.*

Adverbs

A   *Write the adverb that corresponds to each of the following adjectives.*

1. 安静 *ānjìng*   _____

2. 清楚 *qīngchu*   _____

3. 大方 *dàfang*   _____

4. 吃力 *chīlì*   _____

5. 慢慢 *mànmàn*   _____

6. 明白 *míngbai*   _____

7. 努力 *nǔlì*   _____

8. 认真 *rènzhēn*   _____

◀ *For more help, see* Introducing adverbs, *page 63.*

B   *Translate the following negative sentences into Chinese.*

1. He doesn't work.

   _____

2. He is not a student.

   _____

3. My older brother did not call me.

   _____

4. The teacher did not see Xiao Li.

   _____

5. Don't listen to him.

   _____

6. I don't watch TV.

_____

7. Don't call me.

_____

8. My friend did not come.

_____

◀ *For more help, see* Introducing adverbs, *page 63.*

Prepositions

A *Complete each of the following sentences with the correct preposition.*

1. 小李是 _____ 中国来的。

   Xiǎo Lǐ shì _____ Zhōngguó lái de.

2. _____ 中学四年里，我交了很多好朋友。

   _____ zhōngxué sì nián lǐ, wǒ jiāo le hěn duō hǎo péngyou.

3. 我们 _____ 这件事情不太清楚。

   Wǒmen _____ zhè jiàn shìqing bú tài qīngchu.

4. 我打了一个电话 _____ 他。

   Wǒ dǎ le yí ge diànhuà _____ tā.

5. 我把哥哥送 _____ 车站。

   Wǒ bǎ gēge sòng _____ chēzhàn.

6. 下午我 _____ 姐姐一起去看了一场电影。

   Xiàwǔ wǒ _____ jiějie yìqǐ qù kàn le yì chǎng diànyǐng.

7. 他 _____ 我借的书还没还。

   Tā _____ wǒ jiè de shū hái méi huán.

8. _____ 这件事，我没意见。

   _____ zhè jiàn shì, wǒ méi yìjiàn.

9. 爸爸坐 _____ 沙发上看电视。

   Bàba zuò _____ shāfā shang kàn diànshì.

10. 这几门课，我 _____ 历史最有兴趣。

    Zhè jǐ mén kè, wǒ _____ lìshǐ zuì yǒu xìngqù.

◀ *For more help, see* Introducing prepositions, *pages 77–78.*

Verbs

A *Turn each of the following statements into a question ending in* 吗 **ma**.

1. 小李是中学生。*Xiǎo Lǐ shì zhōngxuéshēng.*

    _____

2. 他喜欢打篮球。*Tā xǐhuān dǎ lánqiú.*

    _____

3. 她会做中国饭。*Tā huì zuò Zhōngguó fàn.*

    _____

4. 我看了那个电影了。*Wǒ kàn le nà ge diànyǐng le.*

    _____

5. 玛丽给我打电话了。*Mǎlì gěi wǒ dǎ diànhuà le.*

    _____

◀ *For more help, see* Introducing questions, *page 84.*

B *Turn each of the following statements into a "yes" or "no" question.*

1. 小李是中学生。*Xiǎo Lǐ shì zhōngxuéshēng.*

    _____

2. 他有哥哥。*Tā yǒu gēge.*

    _____

3. 她看中国电影。*Tā kàn Zhōngguó diànyǐng.*

    _____

4. 小王喜欢听音乐。*Xiǎo Wáng xǐhuan tīng yīnyuè.*

    _____

5. 玛丽想到公园去。*Mǎlì xiǎng dào gōngyuán qù.*

    _____

◀ *For more help, see* Introducing questions, *pages 84–85.*

C *Complete each of the following sentences with the correct form of the verb in parentheses, using Verb,* 在 **zài** *+ Verb, or Verb +* 着 **zhe**.

1. 我弟弟每天都 _____中文报纸。(看)

    Wǒ dìdi měitiān dōu _____ Zhōngwén bàozhǐ. (kàn)

2. 她总是六点 _____ 床。(起)

   Tā zǒngshì liù diǎn _____ chuáng. (qǐ)

3. 你为什么 _____ 那张照片？(拿)

   Nǐ wèishénme _____ nà zhāng zhàopiàn? (ná)

4. 玛丽在做什么？她 _____ 歌。(唱)

   (chàng) Mǎlì zài zuò shénme? Tā _____ gē. (chàng)

5. 小李 _____ 一顶帽子。(戴)

   (dài) Xiǎo Lǐ _____ yì dǐng màozi. (dài)

6. 他 _____ 觉，我们小声一点儿。(睡)

   Tā _____ jiào, wǒmen xiǎoshēng yì diǎnr. (shuì)

7. 爸爸平常八点 _____ 班。(上)

   Bàba píngcháng bā diǎn _____ bān. (shàng)

8. 他一天 _____ 八个钟头。(工作)

   Tā yì tiān _____ bā ge zhōngtóu. (gōngzuò)

◀ *For more help, see* Present-time actions and states, *pages 91 and 93.*

D *Complete each of the following sentences with the correct form of the verb in parentheses, using Verb, Verb +* 了 *le,* 在 *zài + Verb, or Verb +* 着 *zhe.*

1. 我打电话给他的时候，他 _____ 功课。(做)

   Wǒ dǎ diànhuà gěi tā de shíhou, tā _____ gōngkè. (zuò)

2. 他上个月 _____ 一辆新车。(买)

   Tā shàng ge yùe _____ yí liàng xīn chē. (mǎi)

3. 昨天她 _____ 不太舒服。(感到)

   Zuótiān tā _____ bú tài shūfu. (gǎndào)

4. 玛丽刚才手里 _____ 书。(拿)

   Mǎlì gāngcái shǒuli _____ shū. (ná)

5. 小李以前 _____ 老师。(是)

   Xiǎo Lǐ yǐqián _____ lǎoshī. (shì)

6. 在昨天的晚会上我 _____ 两杯啤酒。(喝)

   Zài zuótiān de wǎnhuì shàng wǒ _____ liǎng bēi píjiǔ. (hē)

7. 你刚才在做什么？我 _____ 书。(看)

   Nǐ gāngcái zài zuò shénme? Wǒ _____ shū. (kàn)

8. 我哥哥昨天 ＿＿＿＿＿＿＿＿＿ 纽约。(去)

   Wǒ gēge zuótiān ＿＿＿＿＿＿＿＿＿ *Niǔyuē.* (*qù*)

   ◀ *For more help, see* Past actions and states, *pages 95 and 97.*

E   *Translate each of the following sentences into Chinese.*

   1. I always get up at six o'clock.

   ＿＿＿＿＿＿＿＿＿＿＿＿＿＿＿＿＿＿＿＿＿＿＿＿＿＿＿＿＿＿＿＿＿

   2. She speaks French.

   ＿＿＿＿＿＿＿＿＿＿＿＿＿＿＿＿＿＿＿＿＿＿＿＿＿＿＿＿＿＿＿＿＿

   3. We waited for an hour.

   ＿＿＿＿＿＿＿＿＿＿＿＿＿＿＿＿＿＿＿＿＿＿＿＿＿＿＿＿＿＿＿＿＿

   4. Where do they work?

   ＿＿＿＿＿＿＿＿＿＿＿＿＿＿＿＿＿＿＿＿＿＿＿＿＿＿＿＿＿＿＿＿＿

   5. I watched a movie last night.

   ＿＿＿＿＿＿＿＿＿＿＿＿＿＿＿＿＿＿＿＿＿＿＿＿＿＿＿＿＿＿＿＿＿

   6. What are you doing now?

   ＿＿＿＿＿＿＿＿＿＿＿＿＿＿＿＿＿＿＿＿＿＿＿＿＿＿＿＿＿＿＿＿＿

   7. She is wearing a white blouse.

   ＿＿＿＿＿＿＿＿＿＿＿＿＿＿＿＿＿＿＿＿＿＿＿＿＿＿＿＿＿＿＿＿＿

   8. They sang a song at the party last night.

   ＿＿＿＿＿＿＿＿＿＿＿＿＿＿＿＿＿＿＿＿＿＿＿＿＿＿＿＿＿＿＿＿＿

   ◀ *For more help, see* Present-time actions and states, *pages 91 and 93,* and Past actions and states, *pages 95 and 97.*

F   *Complete each of the following sentences with the correct future form of the verb in parentheses, using* 要 + *Verb,* 会 + *Verb,* (会)在 + *Verb, or* 会 + *Verb* + 着.

   1. 我下午＿＿＿＿＿＿＿＿＿ 功课，不能去找你。(做)

      Wǒ xiàwǔ ＿＿＿＿＿＿＿＿＿ *gōngkè, bù néng qù zhǎo nǐ.* (*zuò*)

   2. 明天 ＿＿＿＿＿＿＿＿＿ 雨吗？(下)

      Míngtiān ＿＿＿＿＿＿＿＿＿ *yǔ ma?* (*xià*)

   3. 那时候我可能 ＿＿＿＿＿＿＿＿＿ 晚饭。(吃)

      Nà shíhou wǒ kěnéng ＿＿＿＿＿＿＿＿＿ *wǎnfàn.* (*chī*)

   4. 我今天有很多事情 ＿＿＿＿＿＿＿＿＿。(做)

      Wǒ jīntiān yǒu hěn duō shìqing ＿＿＿＿＿＿＿＿＿. (*zuò*)

5. 你不读书，明天的考试怎么 _____ 得好呢？(考)

   Nǐ bù dú shū, míngtiān de kǎoshì zěnme _____ de hǎo ne? (kǎo)

6. 明天我 _____ 一顶红帽子，你很容易就可以找到我。(戴)

   Míngtiān wǒ _____ yì dǐng hóng màozi, nǐ hěn róngyì jiù kěyǐ zhǎo dào wǒ. (dài)

7. 你什么时候 _____ 加州？(去)

   Nǐ shénme shíhou _____ Jiāzhōu? (qù)

8. 我以后 _____ 很多钱。(有)

   Wǒ yǐhòu _____ hěn duō qián. (yǒu)

   ◀ *For more help, see* Future actions and states, *pages 99 and 101.*

G *Complete each of the following conditional sentences, using the English in parentheses.*

1. 要是我有时间，_____。(I'll go visit you)

   Yàoshi wǒ yǒu shíjiān, _____.

2. 如果你作业写完了，_____。(you can turn it in now)

   Rúguǒ nǐ zuòyè xiě wán le, _____.

3. _____，我们就一起去。(If he arrives by six o'clock)

   _____, *wǒmen jiù yìqǐ qù.*

4. _____，我们就买一张CD吧。(If you like this music)

   _____, *wǒmen jiù mǎi yì zhāng CD ba.*

5. 要是我知道你不在家，_____。(I wouldn't have come)

   Yàoshi wǒ zhīdào nǐ bú zài jiā, _____.

6. 要是早知道这家餐馆不好，_____。(we would have gone elsewhere)

   Yàoshi zǎo zhīdào zhè jiā cānguǎn bù hǎo, _____.

7. _____，我会买一辆车。(If I have lots of money)

   _____, *wǒ huì mǎi yí liàng chē.*

8. 如果你不喜欢他，_____。(don't go to the movies with him)

   Rúguǒ nǐ bù xǐhuan tā, _____.

   ◀ *For more help, see* Conditional sentences, *page 103.*

H *Complete each the following sentences with the correct form of the verb in parentheses, using Verb + 过 guò, Verb + 了 le, or Verb + 完 wán.*

1. 我以前 ＿＿＿＿＿＿ 这个故事了。(听)

   Wǒ yǐqián ＿＿＿＿＿＿ zhè ge gùshi le. (tīng)

2. 我已经 ＿＿＿＿＿＿ 三杯可乐了？(喝)

   Wǒ yǐjīng ＿＿＿＿＿＿ sān bēi kělè le. (hē)

3. 我到他家的时候，他已经 ＿＿＿＿＿＿ 功课了。(做)

   Wǒ dào tā jiā de shíhou, tā yǐjīng ＿＿＿＿＿＿ gōngkè le. (zuò)

4. 你曾经 ＿＿＿＿＿＿ 北京吗？(去)

   Nǐ céngjīng ＿＿＿＿＿＿ Běijīng ma? (qù)

5. 老师说 ＿＿＿＿＿＿ 试以后我们就可以回家。(考)

   Lǎoshī shuō ＿＿＿＿＿＿ shì yǐhòu wǒmen jiù kěyǐ huí jiā. (kǎo)

6. 你 ＿＿＿＿＿＿ 一个钟头了，休息一下吧。(说)

   Nǐ ＿＿＿＿＿＿ yí ge zhōngtóu le, xiūxi yí xià ba. (shuō)

7. 我 ＿＿＿＿＿＿ 三道题了，还有两道题。(做)

   ＿＿＿＿＿＿ sān dào tí le, hái yǒu liǎng dào tí. (zuò)

8. 我 ＿＿＿＿＿＿ 这个人，他是一位医生。(见)

   ＿＿＿＿＿＿ zhè ge rén, tā shì yí wèi yīshēng. (jiàn)

◄ *For more help, see* Completion by the present time, *pages 105 and 107, and* Completion in the past, *page 111.*

I *Translate each of the following sentences into Chinese.*

1. Xiao Li has been online (上网 *shàngwǎng*) in the afternoon.

   ＿＿＿＿＿＿＿＿＿＿＿＿＿＿＿＿＿＿＿＿＿＿＿＿＿＿＿＿

2. Before you came, I had been thinking of you.

   ＿＿＿＿＿＿＿＿＿＿＿＿＿＿＿＿＿＿＿＿＿＿＿＿＿＿＿＿

3. I have been studying Chinese for two years.

   ＿＿＿＿＿＿＿＿＿＿＿＿＿＿＿＿＿＿＿＿＿＿＿＿＿＿＿＿

4. Since my younger brother left, I have been keeping his letters.

   ＿＿＿＿＿＿＿＿＿＿＿＿＿＿＿＿＿＿＿＿＿＿＿＿＿＿＿＿

5. Before you came home, he had been doing his homework.

   ＿＿＿＿＿＿＿＿＿＿＿＿＿＿＿＿＿＿＿＿＿＿＿＿＿＿＿＿

6. Mary has been working for 10 years.

   ＿＿＿＿＿＿＿＿＿＿＿＿＿＿＿＿＿＿＿＿＿＿＿＿＿＿＿＿

7. By midnight, we had been dancing for three hours.

   _____

8. Since this afternoon (till now), he has been sleeping.

   _____

9. She has been singing for an hour.

   _____

10. When the letter came, I had been waiting for three days.

   _____

◀ *For more help, see* Continuation from past to present, *pages 108–109, and* Continuation from past to past, *pages 113 and 115.*

J   *Complete each of the following sentences, using the English phrases in parentheses and imparting the sense of completion in the future or continuation from past to future.*

1. 到明天早上八点，我就已经 _____。(work for 20 hours)

   Dào míngtiān zǎoshang bā diǎn, wǒ jiù yǐjīng _____.

2. 你等一下打电话来的时候，_____。(finish my dinner)

   Nǐ děng yíxià dǎ diànhuà lái de shíhou, _____.

3. 到明年毕业的时候，_____。(live here for four years)

   Dào míngnián bìyè de shíhou, _____.

4. 到明天考试的时候，_____。(study for three days)

   Dào míngtiān kǎoshì de shíhou, _____.

5. 等你回来的时候，_____。(buy that car)

   Děng nǐ huílái de shíhou, _____.

◀ *For more help, see* Completion in the future, *page 117, and* Continuation from past to future, *pages 118–119.*

APPENDIX A
Measure words

When a noun occurs with a numeral or a demonstrative adjective, a measure word is required between them. A measure word (designated MW in the English translations below) indicates the quantity or a permanent quality of the noun it precedes.

三本书	*sān **běn** shū*	three MW books
那本书	*nà **běn** shū*	that MW book

In these examples, the measure word 本 *běn* indicates that the following noun is a bound volume.

There are several types of measure words, including individual classifiers, words referring to containers, words referring to measurement, and words referring to a collection of objects. Of these types, individual classifiers have no equivalent in English.

1. **Individual classifiers**. These measure words, which occur with countable nouns, are of two subtypes: general and specific.

    a. A general classifier, 个 *ge,* which occurs with nouns that do not have specific classifiers

一个人	*yí **ge** rén*	one MW person
五个玩具	*wǔ **ge** wánjù*	five MW toys

    b. Specific classifiers, which are specific to the objects they measure

三本书	*sān **běn** shū*	three MW books
一张桌子	*yì **zhāng** zhuōzi*	one MW table

    See Appendix B (page 147) for a list of common individual classifiers.

2. **Container words**. These occur with countable and mass nouns.

一盒糖果	*yì **hé** tángguǒ*	a **box** of candy

3. **Measurement words**. These occur with countable and mass nouns.

两磅苹果	*liǎng **bàng** píngguǒ*	two **pounds** of apples

4. **Collective words**. These occur with nouns that refer to a collection of objects.

一套家具	*yí **tào** jiājù*	a **suite** of furniture

APPENDIX B
Common individual classifiers

CLASSIFIER		THINGS IT REFERS TO	EXAMPLES
把	*bǎ*	objects with a handle	椅子 *yǐzi* chair, 伞 *sǎn* umbrella
班	*bān*	classes, scheduled services	学生 *xuésheng* student, 车 *chē* scheduled bus
本	*běn*	books, bound volumes	书 *shū* book, 词典 *cídiǎn* dictionary
部	*bù*	works of literature, films, vehicles	电影 *diànyǐng* movie, 车 *chē* car
层	*céng*	floors	楼 *lóu* floor
场	*chǎng*	events of short duration	音乐会 *yīnyuèhuì* concert, 球赛 *qiúsài* ball game
顶	*dǐng*	hats, objects with a protruding top	帽子 *màozi* hat, 帐篷 *zhàngpéng* tent
份	*fèn*	gifts, newspapers	礼物 *lǐwù* gift, 报纸 *bàozhǐ* newspaper
封	*fēng*	objects that can be sealed	信 *xìn* letter
个	*ge*	people, places, and items without specific classifiers	人 *rén* person, 地方 *dìfang* place, 问题 *wèntí* question
根	*gēn*	long, thin objects	绳子 *shéngzi* rope, 香蕉 *xiāngjiāo* banana
架	*jià*	machines, vehicles	飞机 *fēijī* airplane
间	*jiān*	rooms	屋子 *wūzi* room, 教室 *jiàoshì* classroom
件	*jiàn*	upper garments	上衣 *shàngyī* coat, 衬衫 *chènshān* shirt, blouse
棵	*kē*	trees, plants	树 *shù* tree, 植物 *zhíwù* plant
颗	*kē*	small, hard objects	纽扣 *niǔkòu* button, 钻石 *zuànshí* diamond
课	*kè*	lessons	课文 *kèwén* lesson
口	*kǒu*	members of a family, objects with an opening	人 *rén* person, 井 *jǐng* well
块	*kuài*	chunky or lumpy objects	石头 *shítou* rock, 肥皂 *féizào* soap
辆	*liàng*	vehicles	汽车 *qìchē* car, 脚踏车 *jiǎotàchē* bicycle
名	*míng*	people	记者 *jìzhě* reporter, 学生 *xuésheng* student
匹	*pǐ*	horses	马 *mǎ* horse
篇	*piān*	articles, chapters	文章 *wénzhāng* article
扇	*shàn*	objects that open and close	门 *mén* door, 窗 *chuāng* window
首	*shǒu*	poems, songs	诗 *shī* poem, 歌 *gē* song
台	*tái*	engines, machines	电视 *diànshì* television, 电脑 *diànnǎo* computer
条	*tiáo*	long, narrow objects	裤子 *kùzi* pants, 绳子 *shéngzi* rope, 河 *hé* river
头	*tóu*	large animals	牛 *niú* cow, 象 *xiàng* elephant
位	*wèi*	respectful classifier for people	老师 *lǎoshī* teacher, 医生 *yīshēng* doctor
张	*zhāng*	objects with a flat surface	桌子 *zhuōzi* table, 相片 *xiàngpiàn* photo
支	*zhī*	long, thin objects	铅笔 *qiānbǐ* pencil, 毛笔 *máobǐ* brush
只	*zhī*	birds, animals	狗 *gǒu* dog, 鸟 *niǎo* bird
座	*zuò*	mountains, bridges, buildings	山 *shān* mountain, 桥 *qiáo* bridge, 大楼 *dàlóu* building

Answer key

Nouns

A

1. 本 *běn*
2. 顶 *dǐng*
3. 张 *zhāng*
4. 件 *jiàn*
5. 盒 *hé*
6. 个 *ge*
7. 个 *ge*
8. 套 *tào*
9. 头 *tóu*
10. 棵 *kē*

B

1. 很多 *hěn duō*
2. 几个 *jǐ ge*
3. 每张 *měi zhāng*
4. 一些 *yì xiē*
5. 很多 *hěn duō*
6. 几把 *jǐ bǎ*
7. 很多 *hěn duō*
8. 一些 *yì xiē*
9. 很多 *hěn duō*
10. 每只 *měi zhī*

Pronouns

A

1. 他是中国人。
   Tā shì Zhōngguó rén.
2. 她住在纽约。
   Tā zhù zài Niǔyuē.
3. 我们是好朋友。
   Wǒmen shì hǎo péngyǒu.
4. 他喜欢她。
   Tā xǐhuan tā.
5. 它有四扇门。
   Tā yǒu sì shàn mén.
6. 我跟他们出去了。
   Wǒ gēn tāmen chūqù le.
7. 你要请她吃饭吗？
   Nǐ yào qǐng tā chī fàn ma?
8. 我看完了。
   Wǒ kànwán le.
9. 他开走了。
   Tā kāizǒu le.
10. 他在给他打电话。
    Tā zài gěi tā dǎ diànhuà.

B

1. 他的 *tā de*
2. 我的 *wǒ de*
3. 我自己 *wǒ zìjǐ*
4. 她的 *tā de*
5. 他自己的 *tā zìjǐ de*
6. 我们的 *wǒmen de*
7. 他自己 *tā zìjǐ*
8. 他们自己 *tāmen zìjǐ*

C

1. 他的 *tā de*
2. 我们的 *wǒmen de*
3. 我的 *wǒ de*
4. 你的 *nǐ de*
5. 她的 *tā de*
6. 你的 *nǐ de*
7. 他们的 *tāmen de*
8. 他们的 *tāmen de*

D

1. 的 *de*
2. 以前工作 *yǐqián gōngzuò*
3. 在街口 *zài jiēkǒu*
4. 要的 *yào de*

5. 我买面包 *wǒ mǎi miànbāo*
6. 开晚会的 *kāi wǎnhuì de*
7. 有兴趣 *yǒu xìngqu*
8. 我们认识 *wǒmen rènshì*

E

1. 这本书贵，那本不贵。
   Zhè běn shū guì, nà běn bú guì.
2. 我的房子在城东边，我妹妹的在西边。
   Wǒ de fángzi zài chéng dōngbian, wó mèimei de zài xībian.
3. 这些餐馆很好，那些更好。
   Zhè xiē cānguǎn hěn hǎo, nà xiē gèng hǎo.
4. 他爱的是她。
   Tā ài de shì tā.
5. 你要那些糕饼还是这些？
   Nǐ yào nà xiē gāobǐng háishì zhè xiē?
6. 我们可以用我的车。玛丽的不够大。
   Wǒmen kěyǐ yòng wǒ de chē, Mǎlì de bú gòu dà.

F

1. 谁 *shéi*
2. 什么 *shénme*
3. 哪一辆 *nǎ yí liàng*
4. 什么 *shénme*
5. 谁 *shéi*
6. 什么 *shénme*
7. 哪几份 *nǎ jǐ fèn*
8. 谁 *Shéi*
9. 什么 *shénme*
10. 谁 *shéi*
11. 什么 *shénme*
12. 谁 *shéi*

Adjectives

A

1. 高高的 *gāogāo de*
2. 干干净净的 *gāngānjìngjìng de*
3. 黑黑的 *hēihēi de*
4. 瘦瘦的 *shòushòu de*
5. 高高大大的 *gāogāodàdà de*
6. 快快乐乐的 *kuàikuàilèlè de*
7. 清清楚楚的 *qīngqīngchǔchǔ de*
8. 安安静静的 *ānānjìngjìng de*

B

1. 小明比小华聪明。
   Xiǎo Míng bǐ Xiǎo Huá cōngmíng.
2. 我姐姐没有我哥哥快乐。
   Wǒ jiějie méiyǒu wǒ gēge kuàilè.
3. 玛丽跟南茜一样大。
   Mǎlì gēn Nánxī yíyàng dà.
4. 这是图书馆里最好的书。
   Zhè shì túshūguǎn lǐ zuì hǎo de shū.
5. 地铁比公共汽车快。
   Dìtiě bǐ gōnggòngqìchē kuài.
6. 他是班上最差的学生。
   Tā shì bānshàng zuì chà de xuésheng.
7. 我的课没有他们的课有意思。
   Wǒ de kè méiyǒu tāmen de kè yǒu yìsi.
8. 我跟我爸爸一样高。
   Wǒ gēn wǒ bàba yíyàng gāo.

C

1. 这个 *zhè ge*
2. 这些 *Zhè xiē*
3. 那家 *nà jiā*
4. 这篇 *Zhè piān*
5. 那位 *Nà wèi*
6. 这些 *Zhè xiē*
7. 那些 *Nà xiē*
8. 那个 *Nà ge*

D

1. 她的老师 *tā de lǎoshī*
2. 我的房子 *wǒ de fángzi*
3. 他的朋友 *tā de péngyǒu*
4. 我们的狗 *wǒmen de gǒu*
5. 他们的车 *tāmen de chē*
6. 你的中文 *nǐ de Zhōngwén*
7. 你们的桌子 *nǐmen de zhuōzi*
8. 我们的餐厅 *wǒmen de cāntīng*

E

1. 谁的 *shèi de*
2. 哪些 *Nǎ xiē*
3. 哪一门课 *Nǎ yì mén kè*
4. 什么 *shénme*
5. 谁的 *shèi de*
6. 哪一本 *nǎ yì běn*
7. 哪些 *Nǎ xiē*
8. 什么 *shénme*
9. 哪一个门 *nǎ yí ge mén*
10. 什么 *shénme*

Adverbs

A

1. 安静地 *ānjìng de*
2. 清楚地 *qīngchu de*
3. 大方地 *dàfang de*
4. 吃力地 *chīlì de*
5. 慢慢地 *mànmàn de*
6. 明白地 *míngbai de*
7. 努力地 *nǔlì de*
8. 认真地 *rènzhēn de*

B

1. 他不工作。
   Tā bù gōngzuò.
2. 他不是学生。
   Tā bú shì xuésheng.
3. 我哥哥没给我打电话。
   Wǒ gēge méi gěi wǒ dǎ diànhuà.
4. 老师没有看见小李。
   Lǎoshī méiyǒu kànjiàn Xiǎo Lǐ.
5. 别听他的话。
   Bié tīng tā de huà.
6. 我不看电视。
   Wǒ bú kàn diànshì.
7. 别给我打电话。
   Bié gěi wǒ dǎ diànhuà.
8. 我的朋友没来。
   Wǒ de péngyǒu méi lái.

Prepositions

A

1. 从 *cóng*
2. 在 *Zài*
3. 对 *duì*
4. 给 *gěi*
5. 到 *dào*
6. 跟 *gēn*
7. 向 *xiàng* OR 跟 *gēn*
8. 关于 *Guānyú* OR 对 *Duì*
9. 在 *zài*
10. 对 *duì*

Verbs

A

1. 小李是中学生吗？
   Xiǎo Lǐ shì zhóngxuéshēng ma?
2. 他喜欢打篮球吗？
   Tā xǐhuan dǎ lánqiú ma?
3. 她会做中国饭吗？
   Tā huì zuò Zhōngguó fàn ma?
4. 你看了那个电影了吗？
   Nǐ kàn le nà ge diànyǐng le ma?
5. 玛丽给你打电话了吗？
   Mǎlì gěi nǐ dǎ diànhuà le ma?

B

1. 小李是不是中学生？
   Xiǎo Lǐ shì bu shì zhōngxuéshēng?
2. 他有没有哥哥？
   Tā yǒu méiyǒu gēge?
3. 她看不看中国电影？
   Tā kàn bu kàn Zhōngguó diànyǐng?
4. 小王喜欢不喜欢听音乐？
   Xiǎo Wáng xǐhuan bu xǐhuan tīng yīnyuè?
5. 玛丽想不想到公园去？
   Mǎlì xiǎng bu xiǎng dào gōngyuán qù?

C

1. 看 *kàn*
2. 起 *qǐ*
3. 拿着 *ná zhe*
4. 在唱 *zài chàng*
5. 戴着 *dài zhe*
6. 在睡 *zài shuì*
7. 上 *shàng*
8. 工作 *gōngzuò*

D

1. 在做 *zài zuò*
2. 买了 *mǎi le*
3. 感到 *gǎndào*
4. 拿着 *ná zhe*
5. 是 *shì*
6. 喝了 *hē le*
7. 在看 *zài kàn*
8. 去了 *qù le*

E

1. 我总是六点起床。
   Wǒ zǒngshì liù diǎn qǐ chuáng.
2. 她说法语。
   Tā shuō Fǎyǔ.
3. 我们等了一个钟头。
   Wǒmen děng le yí ge zhōngtóu.
4. 他们在哪儿工作？
   Tāmen zài nǎr gōngzuò?
5. 昨天晚上我看了一个电影。
   Zuótiān wǎnshàng wǒ kàn le yí ge diànyǐng.
6. 你现在在做什么？
   Nǐ xiànzài zài zuò shénme?
7. 她穿着一件白衬衫。
   Tá chuān zhe yí jiàn bái chènshān.
8. 昨天晚上他们在晚会上唱了一首歌。
   Zuótiān wǎnshang tāmen zài wǎnhuì shàng chàng le yì shǒu gē.

F

1. 要做　*yào zuò*
2. 会下　*huì xià*
3. 在吃　*zài chī*
4. 要做　*yào zuò*
5. 会考　*huì kǎo*
6. 会戴着　*huì dài zhe*
7. 要去　*yào qù*
8. 会有　*huì yǒu*

G

1. 我就去看你
   wǒ jiù qù kàn nǐ
2. 现在就可以交上来
   xiànzài jiù kěyǐ jiāo shàng lái
3. 要是他六点以前到
   Yàoshi tā liù diǎn yǐqián dào
4. 要是你喜欢这个音乐
   Yàoshi nǐ xǐhuan zhè ge yīnyuè
5. 我就不会来了
   wǒ jiù bú huì lái le
6. 我们就去别家了
   wǒmen jiù qù bié jiā le
7. 要是我有很多钱
   Yàoshi wǒ yǒu hěn duō qián
8. 别跟他去看电影
   bié gēn tā qù kàn diànyǐng

H

1. 听过　*tīng guò*
2. 喝了　*hē le*
3. 做完　*zuò wán*
4. 去过　*qù guò*
5. 考完　*kǎo wán*
6. 说了　*shuō le*
7. 做了　*zuò le*
8. 见过　*jiàn guò*

I

1. 小李下午一直在上网。
   Xiǎo Lǐ xiàwù yìzhí zài shàng wǎng.
2. 你来以前，我一直在想你。
   Nǐ lái yǐqián, wǒ yìzhí zài xiǎng nǐ.
3. 我学中文学了两年了。
   Wǒ xué Zhōngwén xué le liǎng nián le.
4. 我弟弟走了以后，我一直留着他的信。
   Wǒ dìdi zǒu le yǐhòu, wǒ yìzhí liú zhe tā de xìn.
5. 你回家以前，他一直在做功课。
   Nǐ huí jiā yǐqián, tā yìzhí zài zuò gōngkè.
6. 玛丽已经工作了十年了。
   Mǎlì yǐjīng gōngzuò le shí nián le.
7. 到半夜的时候，我们跳舞已经跳了三个钟头了。
   Dào bànyè de shíhou, wǒmen tiàowǔ yǐjīng tiào le sān ge zhōngtóu le.
8. 从下午到现在，他一直在睡觉。
   Cóng xiàwǔ dào xiànzài, tā yìzhí zài shuìjiào.
9. 她唱了一个钟头了。
   Tā chàng le yí ge zhōngtóu le.
10. 信到的时候，我已经等了三天了。
    Xìn dào de shíhou, wǒ yǐjīng děng le sān tiān le.

J

1. 工作了二十个钟头了
   gōngzuò le èrshí ge zhōngtóu le
2. 我就已经吃过晚饭了
   wǒ jiù yǐjīng chī guò wǎnfàn le
3. 我就已经在这儿住了四年了
   wǒ jiù yǐjīng zài zhèr zhù le sì nián le
4. 我就已经学习了三天了
   wǒ jiù yǐjīng xuéxí le sān tiān le
5. 我就已经买了那辆车了
   wǒ jiù yǐjīng mǎi le nà liàng chē le

Lightning Source UK Ltd.
Milton Keynes UK
UKHW052104090719
345819UK00004B/40/P